THE SCHOOL MATHEMATICS PROJECT

When the S.M.P. was founded in 1961, its objective was to devise radically new mathematics courses, with accompanying G.C.E. syllabuses and examinations, which would reflect, more adequately than did the traditional syllabuses, the up-to-date nature and usages of mathematics.

The first stage of this objective is now more or less complete. *Books 1–5* form the main series of pupils' texts, starting at the age of 11+ and leading to the O-level examination in 'S.M.P. Mathematics', while *Books 3T, 4* and *5* give a three-year course to the same O-level examination. (*Books T* and *T4*, together with their Supplement, represent the first attempt at this three-year course, but they may be regarded as obsolete.) *Advanced Mathematics Books 1–4* cover the syllabus for the A-level examination in 'S.M.P. Mathematics' and in preparation are five (or more) shorter texts covering the material of various sections of the A-level examination in 'S.M.P. Further Mathematics'. There are two books for 'S.M.P. Additional Mathematics' at O-level. Every book is accompanied by a Teacher's Guide.

For the convenience of schools, the S.M.P. has an arrangement whereby its examinations are made available by every G.C.E. Examining Board, and it is most grateful to the Secretaries of the eight Boards for their cooperation in this. At the same time, most Boards now offer their own syllabuses in 'modern mathematics' for which the S.M.P. texts are suitable.

By 1967, it had become clear from experience in comprehensive schools that the mathematical content of the S.M.P. texts was suitable for a much wider range of pupil than had been originally anticipated, but that the presentation needed adaptation. Thus it was decided to produce a new series, *Books A–H*, which could serve as a secondary school course starting at the age of 11+. These books are specially suitable for pupils aiming at a C.S.E. examination; however, the framework of the C.S.E. examinations is such that it is inappropriate for the S.M.P. to offer its own examination as it does for the G.C.E.

The completion of all these books does not mean that the S.M.P. has no more to offer to the cause of curriculum research. The team of S.M.P. writers, now numbering some thirty school and university mathematicians, is continually testing and revising old work and preparing for new. At the same time, the effectiveness of the S.M.P.'s work depends, as it always has done, on obtaining reactions from active teachers—and also from pupils—in the classroom. Readers of the texts can therefore send their comments to the S.M.P. in the knowledge that they will be warmly welcomed.

Finally, the year-by-year activity of the S.M.P. is recorded in the annual Director's Reports which readers are encouraged to obtain on request to the S.M.P. Office at Westfield College, University of London, London N.W.3.

ACKNOWLEDGEMENTS

The principal authors, on whose contributions the S.M.P. texts are largely based, are named in the annual Reports. Many other authors have also provided original material, and still more have been directly involved in the revision of draft versions of chapters and books. The Project gratefully acknowledges the contributions which they and their schools have made.

This book—*Book C*—has been written by

Joyce Harris	R. A. Parsons
D. A. Hobbs	C. Richards
K. Lewis	R. W. Strong

and edited by Elizabeth Evans.

We would especially thank Dr J. V. Armitage for the advice he has given on the fundamental mathematics of the course, also, P. G. Bowie for his help in the development of this book.

The drawings at the chapter opening in this book are by Penny Wager.

We are grateful to Denys Fisher (Spirograph) Ltd. Boston Spa, Yorks for providing the Spirograph diagrams and for permission to reproduce them.

We are much indebted to the Cambridge University Press for their cooperation and help at all times in the preparation of this book.

The Project owes a debt to Miss A. Deutsch, Miss J. Sinfield and Mrs J. Whittaker for their assistance and for their typing in connection with this book.

THE SCHOOL MATHEMATICS PROJECT

BOOK C

CAMBRIDGE
AT THE UNIVERSITY PRESS

1969

Published by the Syndics of the Cambridge University Press
Bentley House, 200 Euston Road, London N.W.1
American Branch: 32 East 57th Street, New York, N.Y.10022

© Cambridge University Press 1969

Library of Congress Catalogue Card Number: 68–21399

Standard Book Number: 521 06955 6

Printed in Great Britain
at the University Printing House, Cambridge
(Brooke Crutchley, University Printer)

Preface

This is the third of eight books designed to cover a course suitable for those who wish to take a C.S.E. Examination on one of the reformed mathematics syllabuses.

The material is based upon the first four books of the O-level series, S.M.P. *Books 1–4*. The connection is maintained to the extent that it will be possible to change from one series to the other at the end of the first year or even at a later stage. For example, having started with *Books A* and *B*, a pupil will be able to move to *Book 2*. Within each year's work, the material has been entirely broken down and rewritten.

The differences between this Main School series and the O-level series have been explained at length in the Preface to *Book A* as have the differences between the content of these two S.M.P. courses and that of the more traditional text.

In this book, *Book C*, the Prelude introduces three transformations which preserve shape and size—translation, reflection and rotation. Translations will be considered again in *Book D*, where we shall use vectors to describe them, while reflection and rotation each have a chapter devoted to them in this book. The reflection chapter begins by drawing on the work done on symmetry in *Book A*. The rotation chapter starts with a series of investigations designed to give pupils practical experience of rotations in both two and three dimensions. It then considers properties of rotation, before going on to determine measures and centres of rotation.

Two-dimensional bilateral and rotational symmetry were met in *Book A*. In this book, the study of symmetry in three dimensions is started with a chapter on planes of symmetry. This chapter begins by considering the reflection of certain objects which have been cut 'in half' and then involves the construction of a number of models to help find planes of symmetry. This practical work is essential if pupils are to learn to visualize three-dimensional space. *Book D* will contain work on rotational symmetry in three dimensions.

In this book, we discuss different ways of representing relations and pupils draw the graphs of simple linear relations in the first quadrant. Then, having already extended the number line by introducing the set of directed numbers, we extend to the whole plane. In this book, also, we combine directed numbers by the operations of addition and subtraction, by first considering shifts along the number line. (Multiplication and division of directed numbers will be dealt with in *Book D*.)

The chapter on journeys revises the work done on bearings and provides practice on combining 'distances and bearings' by drawing. This combination of translations will be taken up again in the vector chapter in *Book D*.

In this course, we have decided not to introduce the use of logarithms, but to use the slide rule as our computational aid. However, for at least the first half of the course, the work and examples used will be such that a slide rule is not necessary for computation. (Indeed, at this stage, we are still working towards a thorough understanding of basic computational skills, wherefore the chapter on multiplication and division of decimals.) In *Book C*, pupils learn how and why a slide rule works and use a home-made one to perform simple multiplications and divisions. In later books, home-made rules incorporating logarithmic graph paper and purchased slide rules will be used.

Apart from rudimentary arithmetic, the branch of mathematics that pupils are most likely to meet and use after they have left school is Statistics. In *Book B* we showed how statistical data could be collected and displayed, and in this book we discuss methods of choosing representive values for this data. As the course continues, we hope to develop further the ability to interpret and criticize the statistics and pseudo-statistics to which we are all exposed today.

Answers to exercises are not printed at the end of this book but are contained in the companion Teacher's Guide which gives a detailed commentary on the pupil's text. In this series, the answers and commentary will be interleaved with the text.

Contents

Contents

Prelude

CHANGE OF POSITION
Experiment 1

Cut a small right-angled triangle from card, so that its other angles are 60° and 30°, lay it on a sheet of paper and draw around the outline:

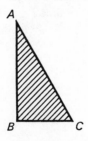

Keep side *AB* on the paper and turn the triangle over, giving:

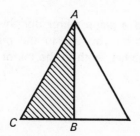

Now keep *CB* on the paper and turn over again. Finally, keep *AB* on the paper and turn over yet once more. Draw and describe the resulting figure.

What other figures or patterns can you make by continuing this sort of process?

Experiment 2

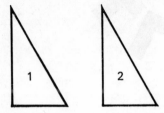

How would you move triangle 1 to the position of triangle 2 keeping it flat on the paper all the time?

Experiment 3

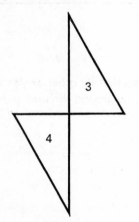

How would you move triangle 3 to the position of triangle 4 keeping it flat on the paper all the time?

Experiment 4

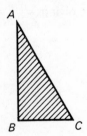

Stand a plane mirror upright on the paper along *AB*. What do you see in the mirror? What do you see altogether, both in the mirror and on the paper?

Experiment 5

Here are some positions which a letter **L** can occupy on a page:

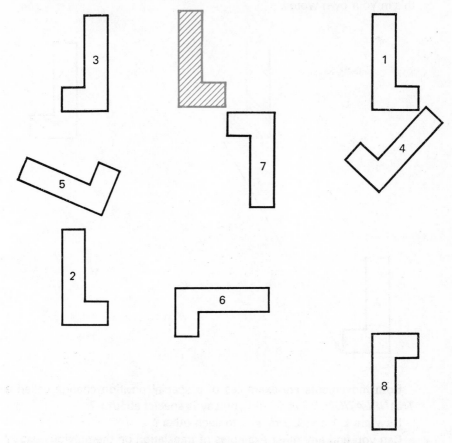

At first sight it might appear that the positions of the letters are scattered in such a way that there is no simple relation between the position of one and the position of another.

We will take the red **L** as the starting position and see how we can get from this one to some of the others.

(*a*) Look at the red **L** and **L** 1.

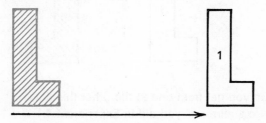

(i) How do you get from one to the other? Describe what happens in your own words.

(ii) What is the simplest way to get from the red **L** to **L** 2? Describe this in your own words.

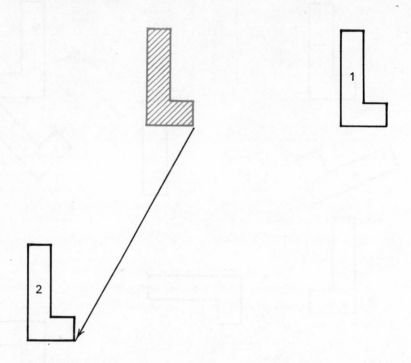

Both movements are examples of a special position change called a *TRANSLATION*. What would you say is special about it?

How are **L** 1 and **L** 2 related to each other?

Can you find any other examples of translation on the previous page? You need not start from the red **L** each time.

(*b*) Next consider the red **L** and **L** 3.

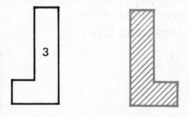

How can you get from one to the other this time?

(*Hint:* use a mirror as you did in Experiment 4.)

What is the relation between the position of the red **L** and **L** 4? Where would you place the mirror this time?

Because we use a mirror to describe these changes of position, we call them *REFLECTIONS*.

Can you find any other examples of reflections of the red **L**?

Describe in your own words how reflection differs from translation.

(*c*) A third type of relation can be found by considering the red **L** and **L** 5.

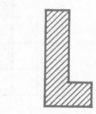

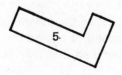

To investigate this, take a piece of tracing paper and trace the outline of the red **L**. Keep the tracing on top of the original and put a pin through at the point *C*. How can you move the tracing of the red **L** onto **L** 5?

5

Try a similar way with the red **L** and **L** 6. In this case you will have to find out where to put the pin.

Both these are examples of *ROTATION*.

(*d*) What is the relation between the red **L** and **L** 7?

(*e*) There remains the relation between the red **L** and **L** 8. Prove to yourself that it cannot be just a simple translation, reflection or rotation.

What is it then? (The full answer to this question will have to wait until after we have made a closer study of translation, reflection and rotation.)

Projects

The **L**'s on page 3 were arranged specially so that easy examples of all the position changes required were present. What would happen if a handful of paper **L**'s were really scattered over a page? If we took one of the shapes as the starting point, would we be able to find translations, reflections and rotations just as easily?

1. Draw an **L** on squared paper.

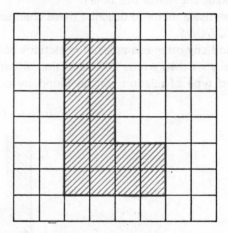

Place this on top of a pile of six or seven pieces of plain paper and cut out a number of equal **L**'s all at once.

Colour the top copy and number all the others (both sides).

Place the coloured **L** in the centre of a large sheet of plain paper and throw the others up from the hand so that they float down and scatter all over the paper.

List the types of position changes you find each time. Is any one type more common than any other? Repeat the experiment many times.

2. Cut out some coloured shapes (they need not be **L**'s) and make a wall display to illustrate position change. What shapes must you avoid if you want to show reflections and rotations properly?

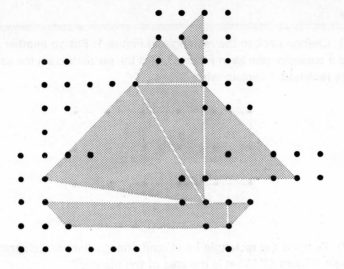

1. Area

1. RECTANGLES, PARALLELOGRAMS, TRIANGLES

1.1 From a rectangle to a triangle

(*a*) Put a rubber band on a pinboard to make the rectangle in Figure 1. What is the area of this rectangle?

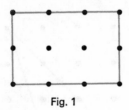

Fig. 1

(*b*) Change the rectangle into the triangle in Figure 2. What is the area of the triangle?

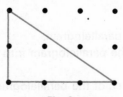

Fig. 2

7

(*c*) Change back to the rectangle in Figure 1. Put on another band to make a parallelogram as in Figure 3. Has the parallelogram the same area as the rectangle? Explain why.

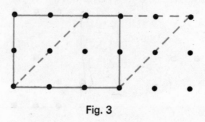

Fig. 3

(*d*) Remove the rectangle band, and change the parallelogram into a triangle (Figure 4). What is the area of the triangle?

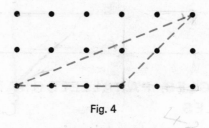

Fig. 4

1.2   From a triangle to a rectangle

(*a*) Make the triangle in Figure 5.

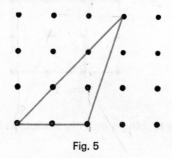

Fig. 5

(*b*) Change it to a parallelogram.

(*c*) Now change the parallelogram into a rectangle. What is the area of this rectangle?

So what was the area of the parallelogram?

So what was the area of the triangle?

Exercise A

1 Set up the rectangle in Figure 6 on a pinboard. Change it to the parallelogram and then to the triangle. What is the area of:

        (*a*) the rectangle,

        (*b*) the parallelogram,

        (*c*) the triangle?

 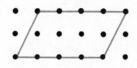 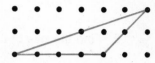

Fig. 6

2 Set up the triangle in Figure 7. Change it to the parallelogram and then to the rectangle. What is the area of:

        (*a*) the rectangle,

        (*b*) the parallelogram,

        (*c*) the triangle?

Fig. 7

3 Using your pinboard, find the area of the triangle in Figure 8.

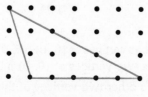

Fig. 8

4 Make the triangle shown in Figure 9 (*a*). Add two more bands as in Figure 9 (*b*). Explain why the area of the triangle is half of the area of the rectangle.

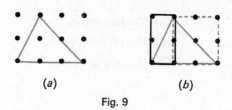

(*a*)   (*b*)

Fig. 9

5 Find the area of the triangle in Figure 10.

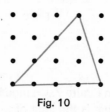

Fig. 10

6 The position of a shape on a pinboard can be given by stating the coordinates of the *vertices* (or corners). For example, two of the vertices in Figure 11 are (1, 1) and (4, 1).

(*a*) Write down the coordinates of the other two vertices.

(*b*) Write down the coordinates of the vertices of a parallelogram which has the same area as the rectangle and has the vertices of its base at (1, 1) and (4, 1).

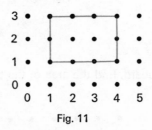

Fig. 11

7 A parallelogram has vertices at (0, 0), (5, 0), (7, 4), (2, 4). A rectangle of equal area has two vertices at (0, 0) and (5, 0).

(*a*) What are the other two vertices of this rectangle?

(*b*) What is the area of the parallelogram?

8   A parallelogram *ABCD* has vertices at *A* (2, 3), *B* (7, 3), *C* (5, 6), *D* (0, 6). Find the other two vertices of rectangles which are equal in area to *ABCD* and which have two vertices at: (*a*) *A* and *B*, (*b*) *C* and *D*.

9   Find the areas of the parallelograms with vertices at:

(*a*)   (0, 0),   (3, 0),   (5, 3),   (2, 3);
(*b*)   (2, 1),   (6, 1),   (4, 3),   (0, 3);
(*c*)   (1, 0),   (3, 0),   (4, 4),   (2, 4);
(*d*)   (1, 1),   (5, 1),   (8, 4),   (4, 4).

10 Find the areas of triangles with vertices at:

(*a*)   (0, 0),   (4, 0),   (3, 4);
(*b*)   (1, 2),   (4, 2),   (3, 4);
(*c*)   (2, 1),   (7, 1),   (6, 6).

2.   MORE POLYGONS

(*a*) Look at Figure 12. How does this triangle differ from the ones in Section 1 ? Try to find its area.

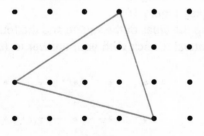

Fig. 12

If you have difficulty, look at Figure 13 where the triangle has been 'boxed in' by another rubber band.
   (i)   What is the area of the rectangle?
   (ii)   What is the area of triangle *A* ?
   (iii)   What is the area of triangle *B* ?
   (iv)   What is the area of triangle *C* ?
   (v)   By taking away the areas of *A*, *B* and *C* from the area of the rectangle, find the area of the triangle.

11

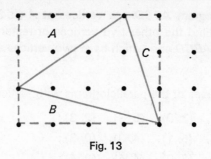

Fig. 13

(*b*) Now try the four-sided shape (*quadrilateral*) in Figure 14. It may help to box it in with a rectangle. What is the area of the quadrilateral?

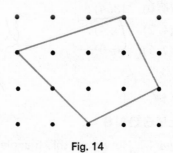

Fig. 14

(*c*) Instead of boxing in the quadrilateral in Figure 14, we can split up its inside (see Figure 15).

By adding up the areas of the square and the four triangles, find the area of the quadrilateral. Check with your answer to (*b*).

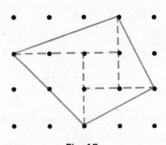

Fig. 15

Exercise B

1 Find the areas of the triangles whose vertices are given by:

(*a*) (1, 2), (3, 5), (5, 4);   (*b*) (2, 5), (4, 3), (6, 7);

(*c*) (1, 1), (5, 0), (4, 4);   (*d*) (1, 2), (7, 1), (8, 4).

2 Find the areas of the quadrilaterals whose vertices are given by:

(a) (1, 2), (4, 0), (7, 2), (5, 4);
(b) (1, 1), (4, 0), (6, 3), (2, 4);
(c) (1, 0), (9, 0), (6, 3), (4, 3).

3 Find the area of the pentagon whose vertices are given by:

(1, 0), (4, 1), (5, 3), (3, 5), (0, 3).

4 Find the area of the octagon whose vertices are given by:

(1, 0), (6, 2), (7, 5), (7, 6), (5, 7), (2, 7), (1, 5), (0, 2).

5 Make a quadrilateral of your own. Find its area and then see if your neighbour can find its area. Repeat for other polygons.

3. AN INVESTIGATION WITH PAPER AND SCISSORS

(a) You may like to write about the work you have been doing. You could do it by cutting out some shapes from coloured sticky paper, and building up a sequence of pictures like Figure 16.

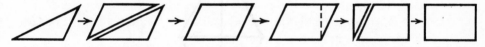

Fig. 16

Explain how this helps you to find the area of a triangle.

(b) By putting two pieces of coloured sticky paper together, cut out two triangles of the same size. Cut one of them into two right-angled triangles and together with the other one, make a rectangle (see Figure 17).

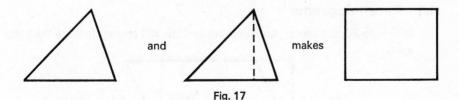

and   makes

Fig. 17

What does this tell you about the area of a triangle? Look back to Exercise A, Question 4, to see how you used a pinboard for this.

13

(*c*) Figure 18 shows a squashed square (its proper name is a *rhombus*).

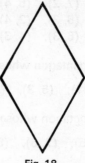

Fig. 18

(i)   How many lines of symmetry has it?
(ii) What is the angle between the lines of symmetry?
(iii) Draw a rhombus on sticky paper, making the diagonals 8 cm and
6 cm. Cut it out, and divide it into four right-angled triangles (Figure 19).
Rearrange these pieces to form a rectangle.
What is the area of the rectangle?
Deduce the area of the rhombus.

Fig. 19

4. AREAS WITHOUT PINBOARDS

4.1 Parallelograms

In Figure 20, the black parallelogram and the red rectangle have the same
area.

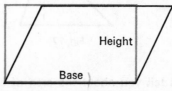

Fig. 20

To find this area you would multiply the length of the base by the height.

(*a*) Find the area of the parallelogram in Figure 21.

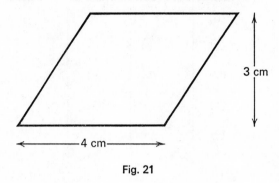

Fig. 21

(*b*) Is it true that the area of the parallelogram in Figure 22 is $3 \times 2 = 6$ cm²?

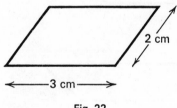

Fig. 22

If you said 'yes', look again. It is the sloping side which is of length 2 cm, not the height. Figure 23 shows this parallelogram again. One of the red dotted lines must be measured for the height.

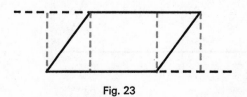

Fig. 23

15

(*c*) Copy the table. Record the lengths of the bases and the heights of the parallelograms in Figure 24 and hence find their areas.

	Base	Height	Area
(i)			
(ii)			
(iii)			
(iv)			
(v)			

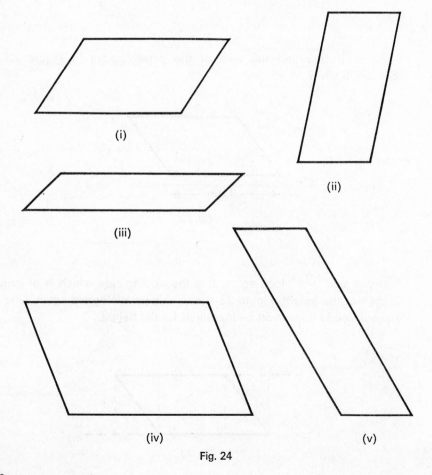

Fig. 24

4.2 Triangles

You have already seen that a triangle is half of a parallelogram, and you know that the area of a parallelogram is found by multiplying the length of the base by the height.

It follows that the area of a triangle is found by multiplying the length of the base by the height, and then dividing by two.

In Figure 25 the triangles are in black, the parallelograms in red, and the heights are shown by dotted red lines.

Copy the table on page 16 again. Measure the lengths of the bases and the heights and hence find the areas of the triangles.

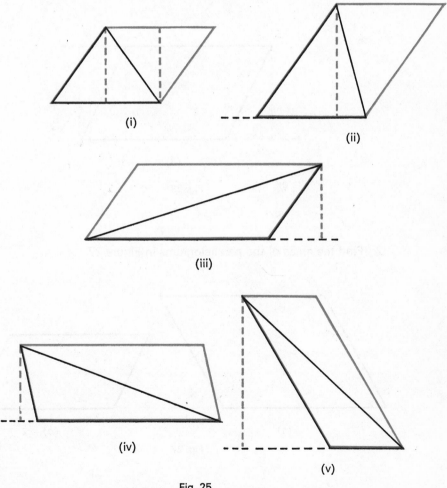

Fig. 25

Exercise C

1   Find the areas of the parallelograms in Figure 26. The heights have been marked in red.

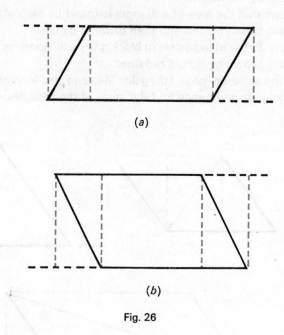

(a)

(b)

Fig. 26

2   Find the areas of the parallelograms in Figure 27.

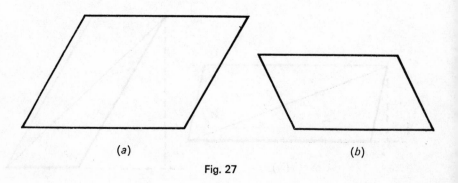

(a)   (b)

Fig. 27

3 Find the areas of the triangles in Figure 28.

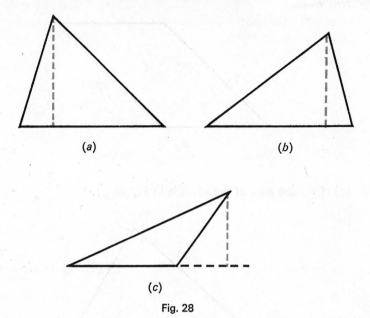

(a)

(b)

(c)

Fig. 28

4 Use your compasses to draw a triangle whose sides have lengths 8 cm, 7 cm, 6 cm. Measure its height and hence find the area.

5 Repeat Question 4 for a triangle whose sides have lengths 6 cm, 7 cm, 12 cm.

6 (a) Find the area of the parallelogram in Figure 29.

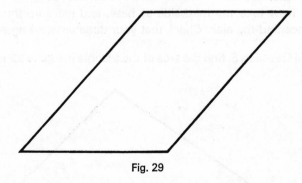

Fig. 29

(b) Now look at it on the side by turning your book so that the side is the base. Measure the new height, and the length of the base. Find the area from these measurements. Check that your answer agrees with (a).

19

7 As in Question 6, find the area of the parallelogram in Figure 30 in two ways.

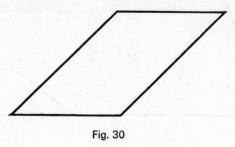

Fig. 30

8 (*a*) Find the area of the triangle in Figure 31.

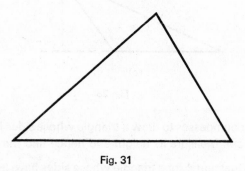

Fig. 31

(*b*) Now turn it on one of its sides. Find its new height, and hence find its area.

(*c*) Now take the third side as base, and measure the new height. Hence find the area. Check that your three answers agree.

9 As in Question 8, find the area of the triangle in Figure 32 in three ways.

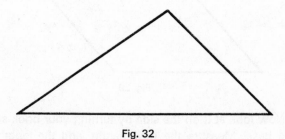

Fig. 32

5. A PINBOARD INVESTIGATION

(a) Figure 33 shows some shapes on a pinboard. Find their areas.

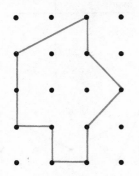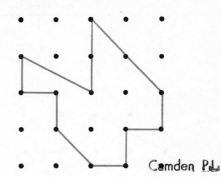

Fig. 33

(b) Make two more shapes yourself and find their areas. Test them on someone else in your class.

(c) Shape A and shape B both have 3 pins inside. Do they have the same area?

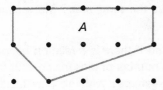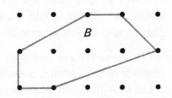

Fig. 34

Shape A has 8 pins on its boundary. How many does B have?

(d) Shape C has the same number of pins on its boundary as shape D. Do they have the same area?

How many pins do they have inside?

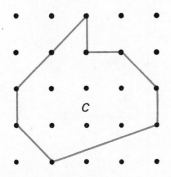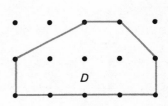

Fig. 35

21

(*e*) Copy and complete this table using Figure 36:

B61	Number of pins on boundary	Number of pins inside	Area
E			
F			

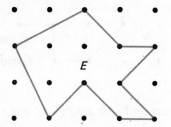 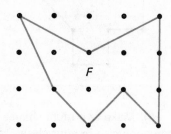

Fig. 36

If two shapes have the same number of pins on their boundaries, and the same number inside, do they have the same area? Make some more shapes and check your answer.

(*f*) Now we are going to try to find if there is a relation between the number of pins on the boundary, the number of pins inside, and the area.

Let's begin with some easy ones—shapes with no pins inside. Find their areas. Record your results in a table.

Number of pins on boundary	Area
3	
4	
5	
6	
7	
8	
.	
.	
.	

What do you notice about the number of pins on the boundary when the area is something-and-a-half?

Try to find a relation between the number of pins on the boundary and the area.

(*g*) Start with 4 pins, say, on the boundary and none inside, and then move your band so that there is just one pin inside, and the same number as before on the boundary.

What is the new area? How has it changed?

Now move the band so that the number on the boundary is the same, and there is another pin inside. How has the area changed? If there were 3 pins inside, and the same number as before on the boundary, what would the area be?

(*h*) If a shape had 8 pins on the boundary and 5 inside, what would its area be? Using your result in (*f*), explain how to find the area if you are told the number of pins on the boundary, and the number of pins inside.

2. Directed numbers

In this chapter we shall be looking at shift numbers. They are called *shift numbers* because they tell us to shift or move along a certain number of places.

A	B	C	D	E	F	G	H	I	J	K	L	M

Fig. 1

1. SINGLE SHIFTS

Suppose you place a counter on the square marked *G* in Figure 1. You could move this counter either to the right or to the left. So a move of 2 could take the counter either to *I* or to *E*. In order to tell the difference between instructions to move to the right and to the left, moves to the right are given by 'blue shifts' (see Figure 2) and moves to the left by 'green shifts' (see Figure 3).

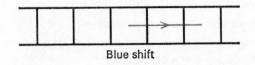

Blue shift

Fig. 2

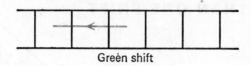

Green shift

Fig. 3

So starting from *G*, a blue 2 tells you to move your counter 2 squares to the right, to *I*, while a green 2 tells you to move your counter 2 squares to the left, to *E*.

(*a*) If you started at *D*, where would your counter be after the shift 'blue 3'?

(*b*) If you started at *H*, where would your counter be after the shift 'green 4'?

Exercise A

1 If you started at *F*, where would your counter be after the following shifts:

(*a*) blue 3;   (*b*) blue 5;   (*c*) green 2;   (*d*) green 4;
(*e*) blue 4;   (*f*) green 5;   (*g*) blue 7;   (*h*) blue 2?

2 If you started at *I*, where would your counter be after the following shifts:

(*a*) green 2;   (*b*) blue 2;   (*c*) green 7;   (*d*) green 1;
(*e*) blue 9;   (*f*) blue 3;   (*g*) green 5;   (*h*) blue 5?

3 If you started at *D*, where would your counter be after the following shifts:

(*a*) blue 4;   (*b*) green 3;   (*c*) blue 5;   (*d*) blue 8;
(*e*) green 1;   (*f*) blue 3;   (*g*) green 2;   (*h*) blue 6?

4 What shift numbers would give the following moves?

(*a*) *J* to *L*;   (*b*) *J* to *F*;   (*c*) *E* to *H*;   (*d*) *B* to *G*;
(*e*) *K* to *G*;   (*f*) *I* to *A*;   (*g*) *C* to *K*;   (*h*) *D* to *C*;
(*i*) *M* to *D*;   (*j*) *F* to *K*.

5 Give 4 different moves your counter could make to obey the shift

(*a*) blue 3;   (*b*) green 6.

6 What name could you give to the shift number which leaves the counter where it is? Is this a blue shift or a green shift?

2. MORE THAN ONE SHIFT

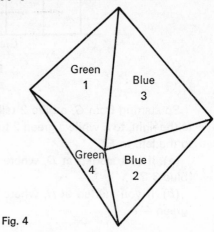

Fig. 4

Make a regular octahedron from card or stiff paper. On its faces mark the numbers 1, 2, 3 and 4 in green, and the numbers 1, 2, 3 and 4 in blue. Copy Figure 5 onto a strip of squared paper.

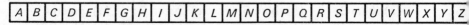

Fig. 5

Now try the following game with your neighbour.

Rules for the Shift Game

Each place a counter (a rolled up strip of paper will do) on the square marked *M*.

Toss a coin to decide who is to go first.

Roll your octahedral die to see how far you can move your counter. For example, your first throw might be blue 3 and so you would move your counter to *P*. Your second throw might be green 4 so you would then move your counter to *L*.

Take turns to throw your die and move your counter. The winner is the person whose counter first comes off the strip at either end.

The game can be improved by using both your own and your neighbour's octahedral die and throwing both dice for each turn. Suppose your counter is on square *D* and you throw green 2 and blue 3; you could move your counter first to *B* and from there to *E*. In what other way could you move your counter? As before, the object of the game is to start at *M* and shift your counter off either end of the alphabetic strip.

2.1 Combining shifts

(*a*)

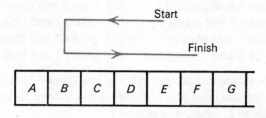

Fig. 6

Suppose your counter is on square *E* and you throw a green 3 and a blue 4. On which square would your counter finally land (see Figure 6)? What single throw would take it to the same place? Try starting from other squares. Is your answer always blue 1?

(*b*)

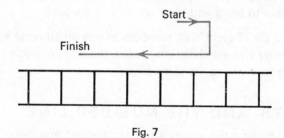

Fig. 7

What single shift number gives the same result as throwing a blue 1 and a green 4 (see Figure 7)?

(*c*)

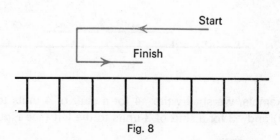

Fig. 8

What single shift number gives the same result as throwing a green 4 and a blue 2 (see Figure 8)?

27

Exercise B

1   What single shift number gives the same result as:

   (*a*) blue 1 and green 3;   (*b*) blue 3 and green 2;
   (*c*) green 3 and green 2;   (*d*) green 2 and blue 4;
   (*e*) blue 1 and blue 2;   (*f*) green 2 and green 4;
   (*g*) blue 3 and green 4;   (*h*) green 1 and blue 3?

2   Suppose your counter was at *L* and you threw a blue 2, taking you to *N*.
    What number must you now throw if you want to 'undo' this; that is,
    go back to *L*, where you started?
    What number would undo

   (*a*) green 3;   (*b*) blue 1;   (*c*) green 2;   (*d*) blue 2?

3   Suppose you made a dodecahedral die marked with the numbers
    1, 2, 3, 4, 5, 6 in green, and the numbers 1, 2, 3, 4, 5, 6 in blue.
    What number would undo

   (*a*) blue 4;   (*b*) green 5;   (*c*) green 6;   (*d*) blue 6?

4   What pairs of shift numbers on the octahedral die that you made, go
    together to bring you back where you started?

5   Find a set of eight shift numbers to put on an octahedral die so that
    whatever two numbers you throw, there is no single number on this
    die to take you to the same place.

3. SHIFTS AND THE NUMBER LINE

In *Book B* we used words such as 'before' and 'after', 'above' and
'below', 'east' and 'west', 'north' and 'south', 'younger' and 'older' to
tell us the direction of other readings from a reference point or zero. We
saw that in all these situations we could use the set of directed numbers
and we shall now use this set to describe shifts to the right and to the left.

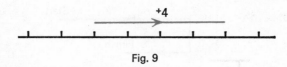

Fig. 9

For example, we shall write ⁺4 for a shift of 4 units to the right (see
Figure 9) and ⁻3 for a shift of 3 units to the left (see Figure 10).

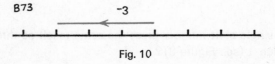

Fig. 10

28

This way of writing shift numbers is connected with the number line, part of which is shown in Figure 11.

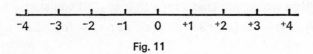

Fig. 11

If we start at 0 each time, the shift ⁺1 takes us to the point ⁺1, the shift ⁺2 to the point ⁺2, the shift ⁺3 to the point ⁺3 and so on. In the same way, each time starting at 0, the shift ⁻1 takes us to the point ⁻1, the shift ⁻2 to the point ⁻2, and so on.

Each point on the number line has come to be called by the name of the shift which, if we start at 0, lands us at that point.

So, for example, ⁻4 means

either (i) a point 4 units to the left of 0, that is the end point of a shift 4 units to the left from 0 (see Figure 12);

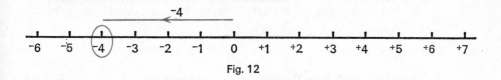

Fig. 12

or (ii) a shift of 4 units to the left not necessarily starting at 0 (see Figure 13).

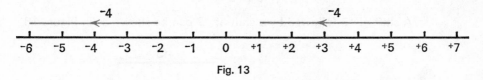

Fig. 13

(a) Start at 0. Where do you land after a shift of ⁺3?

(b) Start at ⁺4. Where do you land after a shift of ⁺3?

(c) Start at ⁻5. Where do you land after a shift of ⁺3?

Exercise C

1 If you started at ⁺2, where would you land after a shift of

(a) ⁺3;   (b) ⁻3;   (c) ⁻5;   (d) ⁺6;   (e) ⁻4?

2 If you started at ⁻3, where would you land after a shift of

(a) ⁺5;   (b) ⁻2;   (c) ⁺2;   (d) ⁻4;   (e) ⁺3?

3 Where would you land after a shift of ⁺3 if you started from

(a) 0;   (b) ⁺3;   (c) ⁻4;   (d) ⁺5;   (e) ⁻2?

4 Where would you land after a shift of ⁻2 if you started from

(a) ⁺4;   (b) ⁻3;   (c) ⁻5;   (d) ⁺2;   (e) ⁺6?

4. COMBINING SHIFTS ON THE NUMBER LINE

We can see how shift numbers are combined by representing them on a number line. For example, we can show a shift of ⁺3 followed by a shift of ⁺2 as in Figure 14.

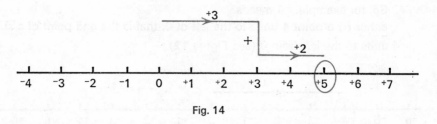

Fig. 14

The single shift from 0 which gives the same result is clearly ⁺5. So a shift of ⁺3 followed by a shift of ⁺2 gives the same result as a shift of ⁺5. This is written for short as

$$^+3 + {}^+2 = {}^+5.$$

A shift of ⁺3 followed by a shift of ⁻7 can be shown as in Figure 15.

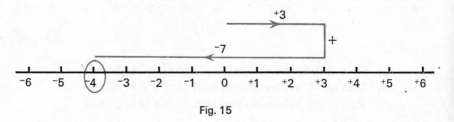

Fig. 15

The single shift from 0 which gives the same result is ⁻4. So a shift of ⁺3 followed by a shift of ⁻7 gives the same result as a shift of ⁻4. This is written as

$$^+3 + {}^-7 = {}^-4.$$

Exercise D

1   By looking at the following number lines (Figure 16), find what single shift number each shows. The first one has been done for you.

(a)

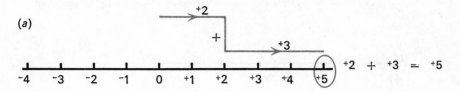

$$+2 \; + \; +3 \; = \; +5$$

(b)

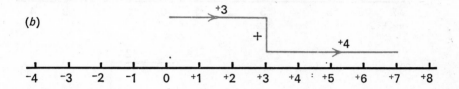

(c)

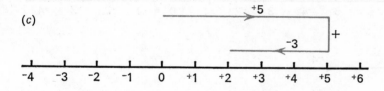

(d)

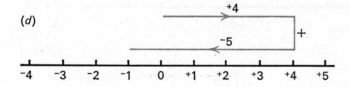

(e)

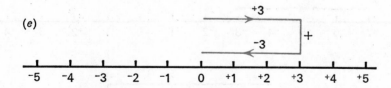

(f)

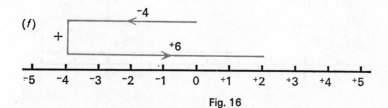

Fig. 16

31

(g)

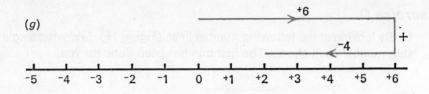

(h)

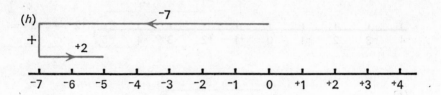

(i)

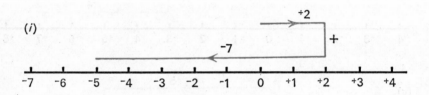

(j)

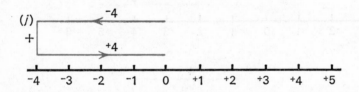

(k)

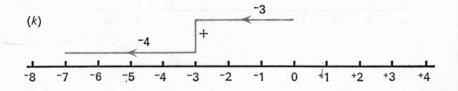

(l)

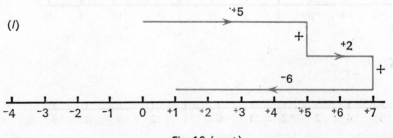

Fig. 16 (*cont.*)

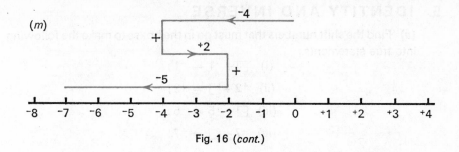

Fig. 16 (*cont.*)

2   By drawing a number line, find what single shift number the following are equal to. The first one has been done for you in Figure 17.

(*a*) $^+3 + ^-5$

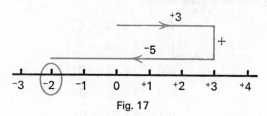

Fig. 17

so $^+3 + ^-5 = ^-2$.

(*b*) $^+2 + ^-6$;	(*c*) $^+3 + ^+4$;	(*d*) $^-5 + ^+2$;
(*e*) $^+2 + ^-5$;	(*f*) $^-4 + ^-2$;	(*g*) $^-2 + ^-4$;
(*h*) $^+2 + ^-2$;	(*i*) $^-3 + ^-3$;	(*j*) $^+3 + ^+2 + ^-7$;
(*k*) $^-3 + ^+4 + ^-5$;	(*l*) $^-2 + ^-3 + ^-4$;	(*m*) $^-5 + ^+5$.

3   Find what shift number fits into the box. The first one has been done for you in Figure 18.

(*a*) $^-5 + \square = ^+3$

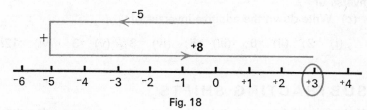

Fig. 18

so $^-5 + ^+8 = ^+3$.

(*b*) $^+4 + \square = ^+7$;	(*c*) $^+5 + \square = ^-1$;
(*d*) $^-3 + \square = ^+5$;	(*e*) $^+6 + \square = 0$;
(*f*) $^-4 + \square = 0$;	(*g*) $^+2 + ^+3 + \square = ^-2$;
(*h*) $^-4 + ^+2 + \square = ^+3$;	(*i*) $^+3 + \square = 0$.

5. IDENTITY AND INVERSE

(*a*) Find the shift numbers that must go in the boxes to make the following into true statements:

$$\text{(i)} \quad \Box + {}^-1 = {}^-1;$$

$$\text{(ii)} \quad {}^+2 + \Box = {}^+2;$$

$$\text{(iii)} \quad \Box + {}^+5 = {}^+5;$$

$$\text{(iv)} \quad {}^-7 + \Box = {}^-7.$$

What is special about the shifts in the boxes?

Any shift remains unchanged when we add the zero shift to it. For example, ${}^-6 + 0 = {}^-6$. We call the zero shift the *identity*.

(*b*) Find the shift numbers that must go in the boxes to make the following into true statements:

$$\text{(i)} \quad {}^-2 + {}^+2 = \Box;$$

$$\text{(ii)} \quad {}^+4 + {}^-4 = \Box;$$

$$\text{(iii)} \quad \Box + {}^-2 = 0;$$

$$\text{(iv)} \quad {}^+3 + \Box = 0;$$

$$\text{(v)} \quad {}^-5 + \Box = 0;$$

$$\text{(vi)} \quad \Box + {}^+7 = 0;$$

$$\text{(vii)} \quad {}^+7 + \Box = 0.$$

What do you notice?

When the result of adding two shifts is the identity, we say that each of these shifts is the *additive inverse* of the other. For example, as

$$^-7 + {}^+7 = 0,$$

we say that ${}^+7$ is the additive inverse of ${}^-7$, and that ${}^-7$ is the additive inverse of ${}^+7$.

(*c*) Write down the additive inverses of:

(i) ${}^-2$; (ii) ${}^+6$; (iii) ${}^-5$; (iv) ${}^-8$; (v) ${}^+3$; (vi) ${}^-12$.

6. SUBTRACTING SHIFTS

We have seen how to 'add' shift numbers by understanding that

$$^+2 + {}^-5$$

means a shift of ${}^+2$ followed by a shift of ${}^-5$.

We shall now try to give a meaning to the 'subtraction' of shift numbers. We know that if we take away something from itself we are always left with nothing. It seems reasonable to expect that this is also true of shift numbers, so

$$^+3 - {}^+3 = 0.$$

But we know from Exercise D that

$$^+3 + {}^-3 = 0,$$

so subtracting $^+3$ gives the same answer as adding $^-3$.
This suggests that $- {}^+3$ means the same as $+ {}^-3$.
We also have

$$^-3 - {}^-3 = 0$$

and

$$^-3 + {}^+3 = 0,$$

so perhaps $- {}^-3$ means the same as $+ {}^+3$.

(*a*) What can you see from the following pairs of statements? The first one has been done for you.

$$\text{(i)} \quad {}^+5 - {}^+5 = 0,$$

$$^+5 + {}^-5 = 0;$$

so $- {}^+5$ means the same as $+ {}^-5$.

(ii) $\quad {}^+7 - {}^+7 = 0,$ (iii) $\quad {}^-4 - {}^-4 = 0,$

$\qquad {}^+7 + {}^-7 = 0;$ $\qquad {}^-4 + {}^+4 = 0;$

(iv) $\quad {}^+2 - {}^+2 = 0,$ (v) $\quad {}^-6 - {}^-6 = 0,$

$\qquad {}^+2 + {}^-2 = 0;$ $\qquad {}^-6 + {}^+6 = 0.$

We see that the idea that $- {}^+3$ means $+ {}^-3$, and $- {}^-3$ means $+ {}^+3$, works when we subtract a number from itself. Does it work when we subtract from other numbers? Let us consider some number patterns.

(*b*) Use the number pattern to copy and complete the following subtractions:

$$^+2 - {}^+2 = \quad 0$$

$$^+3 - {}^+2 = {}^+1$$

$$^+4 - {}^+2 =$$

$$^+5 - {}^+2 =$$

$$^+6 - {}^+2 = {}^+4$$

$$^+7 - {}^+2 =$$

$$^+8 - {}^+2 = \quad .$$

Since the shift number from which we subtract $^+2$ is one unit larger each time, it seems reasonable to expect that the answers will also be one unit larger each time.

(c) Use the number pattern to copy and complete the subtractions on the left of the page and then compare them with the additions on the right.

$^+4 - {}^+4 = 0$	$^+4 + {}^-4 = 0$
$^+4 - {}^+3 = {}^+1$	$^+4 + {}^-3 = {}^+1$
$^+4 - {}^+2 =$	$^+4 + {}^-2 = {}^+2$
$^+4 - {}^+1 =$	$^+4 + {}^-1 = {}^+3$
$^+4 - 0 =$	$^+4 + 0 = {}^+4$
$^+4 - {}^-1 =$	$^+4 + {}^+1 = {}^+5$
$^+4 - {}^-2 =$	$^+4 + {}^+2 = {}^+6$
$^+4 - {}^-3 =$	$^+4 + {}^+3 = {}^+7.$

From these examples we now see that, *instead of subtracting a shift number, we can add its additive inverse.* We shall assume that this statement is always true.

Example 1

Find $^+5 - {}^-1$.

$- {}^-1$ means the same as $+ {}^+1$.

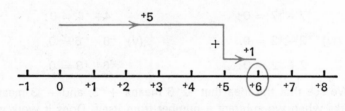

Fig. 19

So $^+5 - {}^-1 = {}^+5 + {}^+1 = {}^+6.$

Exercise E

1 Find the following with as little working as possible:

(a) $^+6 - {}^+4$;   (b) $^+5 - {}^-7$;   (c) $^+8 - {}^+4$;

(d) $^+3 - {}^+8$;   (e) $^-5 - {}^+4$;   (f) $^-6 - {}^-5$;

(g) $^-3 - {}^-9$;   (h) $^-5 - {}^+5$;   (i) $^+8 - {}^+8$;

(j) $^+5 - {}^+3$;   (k) $^-2 - {}^-4$;   (l) $^+3 - {}^-5$;

(m) $^-4 - {}^+1$;   (n) $^-12 - {}^-20$.

2 Find the shift numbers that must go in the boxes to make the following into true statements. (The first one has been done for you.)

(a) $\square - {}^-3 = {}^+5$

$\qquad {}^-{}^-3$ means the same as $+ {}^+3$

$\square + {}^+3 = {}^+5$

so $\qquad \square = {}^+2.$

(b) $\square - {}^-5 = {}^+7;$ (c) $\square - {}^+5 = {}^+2;$

(d) $\square - {}^-2 = {}^-2;$ (e) $\square - {}^+3 = {}^+1;$

(f) $\square - {}^-4 = {}^+3;$ (g) $\square - {}^+1 = {}^-4;$

(h) $\square - {}^-2 = {}^+6;$ (i) $\square - {}^+2 = {}^-2;$

(j) $\square - {}^+5 = {}^-1;$ (k) $\square - {}^-5 = {}^-2.$

3

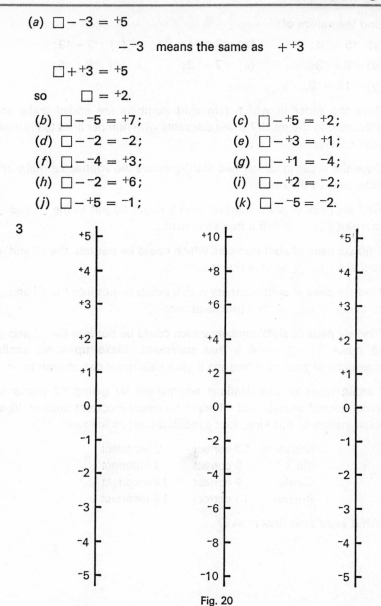

Fig. 20

Figure 20 shows a nomogram for adding and subtracting, a device you have met before. By putting a ruler across the positive numbers see if you can remember how to add and subtract. Now use the same methods to add and subtract some of the shift numbers given in Exercise D and Question 1 of this exercise. Do the answers you get agree with the ones you got previously?

4   Find the values of:

(a) $^+5 + {}^+8$;   (b) $^+3 + {}^+4$;   (c) $^+2 - {}^+9$;

(d) $^-6 + {}^+3$;   (e) $^-7 - {}^-2$;   (f) $^-8 + {}^-6$;

(g) $^-13 - {}^-3$.

5   Does the order in which two shift numbers are added make any difference to the result? Draw diagrams with number lines to illustrate your answer.

6   Does the order in which two shift numbers are subtracted make any difference to the result?

7   Find six pairs of shift numbers which could be put in the □ and △ to make □ + △ = $^+8$ a true statement.

8   Find six pairs of shift numbers which could be put into the □ and △ to make □ + △ = $^+1$ a true statement.

9   Find six pairs of shift numbers which could be put into the □ and △ to make □ + △ = $^-3$ a true statement.

10 Find six pairs of shift numbers which could be put into the □ and △ to make □ − △ = $^+4$ a true statement. Make up some similar questions of your own and see if your neighbour can answer them.

11 Certain types of examinations are marked by giving $^+2$ marks for every correct answer and $^-1$ mark for every incorrect answer. In an examination of this kind, four candidates did as follows:

Adrian	10 correct	9 incorrect
Bill	8 correct	3 incorrect
Carole	9 correct	11 incorrect
Doreen	13 correct	14 incorrect.

What were their final marks?

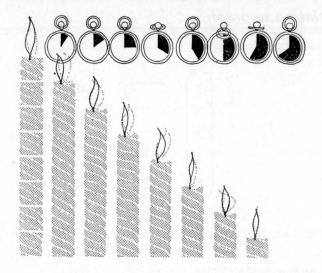

3. From relation to graph

1. REPRESENTING RELATIONS

Consider a fairground big wheel which is steadily turning. Do you think there is any connection between the number of turns the wheel has made and the time it has been moving?

Suppose that a man was timing the big wheel after it had started moving,

and at the end of 1 minute it had made 3 turns,

and at the end of 2 minutes it had made 6 turns.

How many turns will it have made at the end of 4 minutes?

If the wheel was moving for 5 minutes the man would have two sets of measurements:

the number of minutes {1, 2, 3, 4, 5} and

the number of turns {3, 6, 9, 12, 15}.

We can represent the relation between these two sets in three ways.

(*a*) as a mapping diagram, shown in Figure 1 :

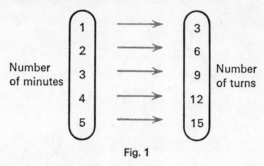

Fig. 1

(*b*) as a set of ordered pairs :
$$\{(1, 3), (2, 6), (3, 9), (4, 12), (5, 15)\};$$

(*c*) as a general statement :
'the number of turns is three times the number of minutes.'

1.1 Mapping diagrams

We can extend the idea of a mapping diagram by representing the members of each set on a number line.

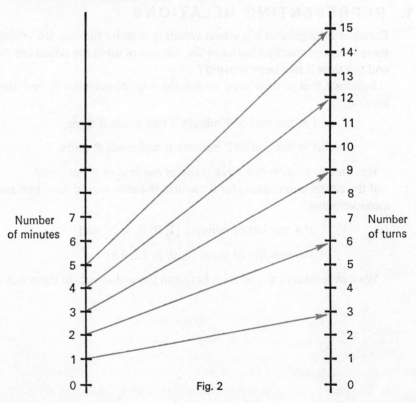

Fig. 2

Figure 2 shows the connection between the number of minutes and the number of turns.

How many turns would be made in $\frac{1}{2}$ minute?

How many turns would be made in 0 minutes?

Can you draw arrowed lines to represent your answers?

How many turns would be made in x minutes?

1.2 Coordinate diagrams

Writing the relation as a set of ordered pairs we have:

$$\{(1, 3), (2, 6), (3, 9), (4, 12), (5, 15)\}.$$

These pairs look like the coordinates of a set of points.

Plot them as coordinates on squared paper (see Figure 3). What happens?

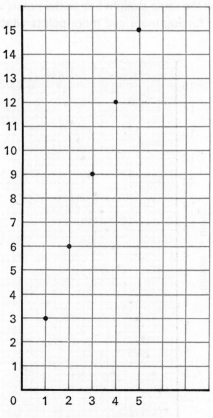

Fig. 3

The points appear to lie on a straight line.

What do the numbers on the axis across the page represent?

What do the numbers on the axis up the page represent?

How many turns would be made in $\frac{1}{2}$ minute? What is the corresponding ordered pair? Can you show it on your squared paper?

Complete the following ordered pairs:

$$(\tfrac{1}{2}, 1\tfrac{1}{2}), \quad (1\tfrac{1}{2}, \quad), \quad (2\tfrac{1}{2}, \quad), \quad (3\tfrac{1}{2}, \quad), \quad (4\tfrac{1}{2}, \quad).$$

Show these on your paper. Do they appear to lie on the same straight line?

How many turns would be made in (a) $\tfrac{1}{4}$ minute, (b) $\tfrac{3}{4}$ minute?

Complete the following ordered pairs:

$$(\tfrac{1}{4}, \tfrac{3}{4}), \quad (\tfrac{3}{4}, 2\tfrac{1}{4}), \quad (1\tfrac{1}{4}, \quad), \quad (1\tfrac{3}{4}, \quad), \quad (2\tfrac{1}{4}, \quad), \quad (2\tfrac{3}{4}, \quad),$$

$$(3\tfrac{1}{4}, \quad), \quad (3\tfrac{3}{4}, \quad), \quad (4\tfrac{1}{4}, \quad), \quad (4\tfrac{3}{4}, \quad).$$

Show these points on your squared paper.

As you can see from Figure 4, we now have many more points and they appear to lie on the same straight line as the points we plotted in Figure 3. We can go on finding more and more points which all appear to lie on this line.

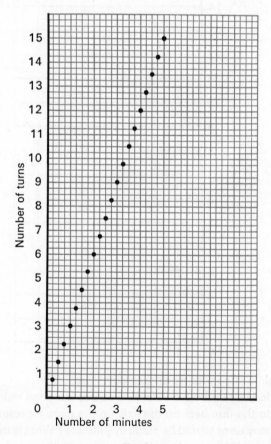

Fig. 4

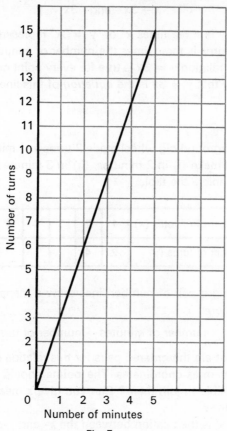

Fig. 5

In fact, we can join up the points by drawing a line with a ruler (see Figure 5). This straight line is called the *graph* of the relation. (Relations whose graphs are straight lines are sometimes called *linear relations*.)

Does the point (0, 0) lie on the line?

Is it true that for every point on the line, the second coordinate is always three times the first coordinate?

If we let x stand for the number of minutes, then the number of turns is $3x$. We can represent the relation by saying

$$x \longrightarrow 3x$$

number of minutes   number of turns

If we think of the ordered pairs as coordinates, and let y stand for the number of turns, then

the x-coordinate is the number of minutes and

the y-coordinate is the number of turns.

So $\qquad x \to 3x$ and $3x = y.$

Therefore, 'y is three times x' or '$y = 3x$' represents the statement 'the number of turns is three times the number of minutes'.

Since the relation $y = 3x$ is true for every point on the line in Figure 5, then we say that $y = 3x$ is the *equation* of this line.

Exercise A

1 If the fairground big wheel made 2 turns in 1 minute, how many turns would it make (i) in 2 minutes, (ii) in 3 minutes?
   (*a*) Complete the table

Number of minutes (x)	1	2	3	4	$\frac{1}{2}$	$1\frac{1}{2}$	$\frac{1}{4}$	0
Number of turns (y)	2	4						

(*b*) Using a pair of number lines draw a mapping diagram to show the relation

number of minutes $\to$ number of turns.

(*c*) What are the ordered pairs for this relation?
   Plot them as coordinates. The points should lie in a straight line. Is it sensible to join them? Can you give a meaning to all the points on the line?
(*d*) What is the relation between the x- and y-coordinates?
(*e*) What is the equation of the line?

2 My brother is two years older than me. For example, when he started school, I was 3 and he was 5. When I started school, I was 5 and he was 7.
   On a pair of number lines, draw a mapping diagram to show

my age $\to$ my brother's age.

What do you notice? How does the mapping diagram differ from the one you drew in Question 1?
   On squared paper, plot some ordered pairs representing this relation. What do you notice?
   If x represents my age and y my brother's age, what is the connection between x and y?

3 A candle, 8 cm high, loses 1 cm of height every hour. After 1 hour it is 7 cm high.
   Find its height after 2 hours, 3 hours, etc.

Draw a mapping diagram to show

number of hours → height of candle.

Find ordered pairs for this relation. Plot them as coordinates.
What do the numbers along each axis represent? What is the relation between them?

2. FINDING RELATIONS

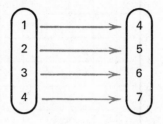

If you are given this mapping diagram, can you find the relation between the two sets of numbers?

You may be able to spot it straight away, but if not, drawing a mapping diagram on number lines may help you (see Figure 6).

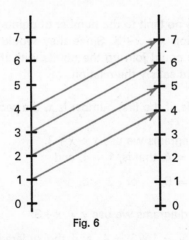

Fig. 6

How does it help you?
Each number is mapped onto the number 3 more than itself. We write this as

$$x \rightarrow x+3.$$

What does x stand for?
The ordered pairs are (1, 4), (2, 5), (3, 6), (4, 7).

45

Plotting these as coordinates we get the points shown in black in Figure 7.

If $x \rightarrow x+3$ and we let x stand for a member of the set of *all* positive numbers, we can find the images of 0, $\frac{1}{2}$, $1\frac{1}{2}$, 5, to get the ordered pairs $(0, 3)$, $(\frac{1}{2}, 3\frac{1}{2})$, $(1\frac{1}{2}, 4\frac{1}{2})$, $(5, 8)$. These are shown in red in Figure 7.

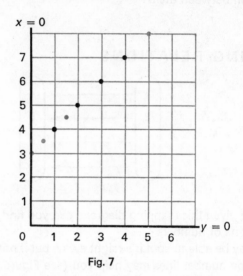

Fig. 7

In fact there is no limit to the number of points that we could plot that satisfy the relation $x \rightarrow x+3$. Since they would all appear to lie on a straight line, we could join up the points with this line and every point on the line would satisfy the relation.

In this example, if the first number is x, the second number is $x+3$ so that $y = x+3$.

In mapping diagrams we use $x \rightarrow x+3$.

So, $1 \rightarrow 1+3 = 4$, that is, $1 \rightarrow 4$, and

$$2 \rightarrow 2+3 = 5, \quad \text{or} \quad 2 \rightarrow 5.$$

In coordinate diagrams we use $y = x+3$.

So, if $x = 1$, $y = 1+3 = 4$, and the ordered pair is $(1, 4)$; and if $x = 2$, $y = 2+3 = 5$, and the ordered pair is $(2, 5)$.

For every point on the line in Figure 7, the y-coordinate is 3 more than the corresponding x-coordinate, or

$$y = x+3.$$

We call this the equation of the line in Figure 7.

Exercise B

1 (a) (0, 1), (1, 2), (2, 3), (3, 4).

These ordered pairs represent a mapping in which

$$0 \to 1,$$
$$1 \to 2,$$
$$2 \to 3,$$
$$3 \to 4.$$

(i) Draw a mapping diagram on two number lines for this relation.
(ii) Find three more ordered pairs which could belong to the set.
(iii) Find the relation between the x- and y-coordinates.

Do the same for the following sets of points:

(b) (2, 0), (3, 1), (4, 2), (5, 3);
(c) (1, 7), (2, 6), (3, 5), (4, 4);
(d) (0, 5), (1, 6), (2, 7), (3, 8);
(e) (1, 1), $(1\frac{1}{2}, 1\frac{1}{2})$, (2, 2), $(2\frac{1}{2}, 2\frac{1}{2})$.

2 In Section 2, $y = x + 3$ is one way of writing the relation between the coordinates. This says 'the y-coordinate is 3 more than the x-coordinate'. But it is also true that 'the x-coordinate is 3 less than the y-coordinate'. This could be written as

$$x = y - 3.$$

A third way is to say that 'the x-coordinate subtracted from the y-coordinate is always 3'. This is written as

$$y - x = 3.$$

Find three ways of writing the relations in each of the parts (a), (b), (c), (d), (e) of Question 1.

3 The following sets of ordered pairs represent a mapping whose graph is a straight line. Find three more ordered pairs which belong to each set and the equation which each set satisfies. Can you write it in more than one way?

(a) (1, 4), (2, 8), (3, 12), (4, 16);
(b) (2, 1), (4, 2), (6, 3), (8, 4);
(c) (0, 5), (1, 4), (2, 3), (3, 2);
(d) (1, 2), (2, 3), (3, 4), (4, 5);
(e) (3, 1), (6, 2), (9, 3), (12, 4).

4   Figure 8 shows the mapping $x \to x - 1$ applied to the set {2, 3, 4, 5, 6}.

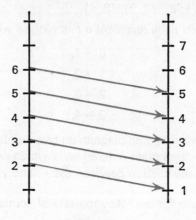

Fig. 8

Draw similar diagrams for each of the following mappings and sets.

(a) $x \to x + 2$, {0, 1, 2, 3, 4, 5};

(b) $x \to x - 3$, {3, 4, 5, 6, 7};

(c) $x \to 4x$, {0, 1, 2, 3};

(d) $x \to \frac{1}{2}x$, {1, 2, 3, 4, 5, 6}.

3. GRAPHS OF RELATIONS

(a) What is the relation between the coordinates of the following ordered pairs?

$$(0, 2), \quad (1, 3), \quad (2, 4), \quad (3, 5).$$

The y-coordinate is 2 more than the x-coordinate.

So $y = x + 2$.

If $x = 4$, what is y?

If $x = 5$, what is y?

What does Figure 9 (opposite) show?

Does the point $(1\frac{1}{2}, 3\frac{1}{2})$ lie on the line with equation $y = x + 2$? Does it satisfy the relation?

Does the point (6, 8) lie on the line? Does it satisfy the relation?

Can you give the coordinates of three more points on the line? Check that they satisfy the relation $y = x + 2$.

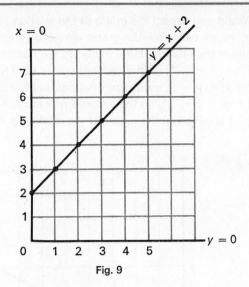

Fig. 9

(*b*) Consider the relation $y = x - 2$.
Can you find some ordered pairs which satisfy this relation?
If $x = 2$, what is y?
If $x = 3$, what is y?
If $x = 4$, what is y?
Check that the following points satisfy the relation:

$(2, 0)$, $(3, 1)$, $(4, 2)$, $(5, 3)$, $(2\frac{1}{2}, \frac{1}{2})$, $(3\frac{1}{2}, 1\frac{1}{2})$, $(8, 6)$.

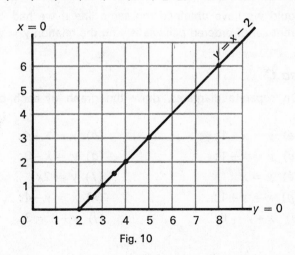

Fig. 10

When we plot these points, we find they lie in a straight line. The graph of the relation $y = x - 2$ is the straight line which passes through these points.

49

(*c*) Would you expect the graph of the relation $y = \frac{1}{2}x$ to be a straight line? Before we can draw the graph we need to find some ordered pairs which satisfy the relation. How many do we need to find?

When $x = 2$, $y = 1$, so the ordered pair is (2, 1).

When $x = 4$, $y = 2$, so the ordered pair is (4, 2).

When $x = 7$, $y = 3\frac{1}{2}$, so the ordered pair is $(7, 3\frac{1}{2})$.

Figure 11 shows that the graph of the relation $y = \frac{1}{2}x$ *is* a straight line.

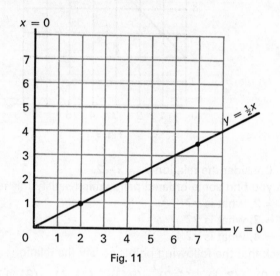

Fig. 11

Would we have obtained the same line if we had chosen to plot a different set of ordered pairs satisfying the relation $y = \frac{1}{2}x$?

Exercise C

1 On separate diagrams, draw the graph of each of the following relations.

(*a*) $y = x+1$; (*b*) $y = x+4$;

(*c*) $y = x-1$; (*d*) $y = x-3$;

(*e*) $y = x$; (*f*) $y = 2x$;

(*g*) $x = y+1$; (*h*) $x = y-4$;

(*i*) $x+y = 6$; (*j*) $x+y = 3$.

4. FURTHER RELATIONS

Investigation 1

On squared paper, complete the addition table in Figure 12 (opposite).

50

10										
9										
8										
7										
6	7									
5	6	7								
4	5	6	7	8						
3	4	5	6	7	8	9				
2	3	4	5	6	7	8	9			
1	2	3	4	5	6	7	8	9	10	
0	1	2	3	4	5	6	7	8	9	10

Fig. 12

Shade in all the eights. What do you notice?
Shade in all the twelves. What do you notice?
(*a*) What is the equation of the line of crosses in Figure 13?

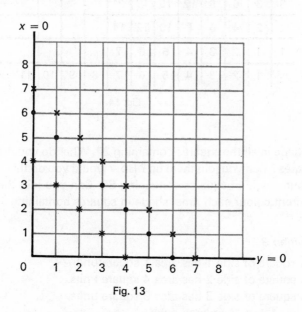

Fig. 13

(*b*) What is the equation of the line of dots?
(*c*) What is the equation of the line of stars?

Investigation 2

On squared paper complete the multiplication square, part of which is shown in Figure 14.

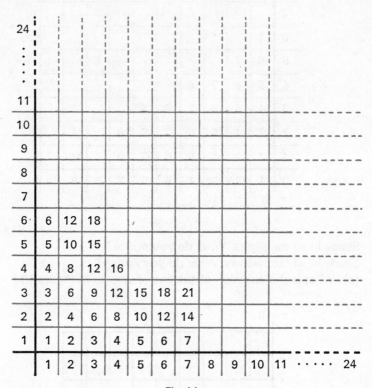

Fig. 14

Shade in all the squares containing 24. What do you notice about these squares? Can you join them up? How would you do this? With a different colour, shade in squares containing 36. Can you join these up? Using a different colour each time, shade in squares containing 18, 12, ...

Investigation 3

A square of side 1 has area 1 square unit.
A square of side 2 has area 4 square units.
A square of side 3 has area 9 square units.
Write these as ordered pairs.
Plot them on squared paper. (Arrange the numbers on your axes as in Figure 15.)

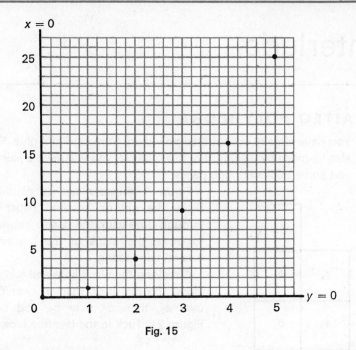

Fig. 15

Can you join them up?
What does this mean?
Can you use your graph to find the side of a square of area 5 square units?

Interlude

PLAITED POLYHEDRA

You have already constructed polyhedra from card and glue. Models can also be made by plaiting. For this method, you will need a pair of scissors and some thick cartridge paper.

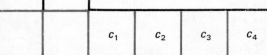

Figure 1 shows a net for plaiting a cube. Draw the net on squared paper and prick through onto cartridge paper. You are advised to make the sides of the squares at least 4 centimetres long.

Cut along the black lines and fold backwards along the red lines. Plait a_1 over b_1, then c_1 over a_2, then b_2 over c_2, and so on (see Figure 2). Tuck in the last free face, b_5.

Fig. 1

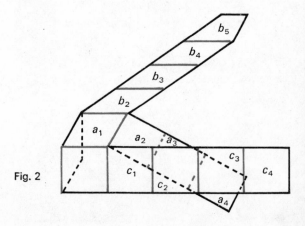

Fig. 2

You will find isometric paper helpful for plaiting the nets for a tetrahedron and an octahedron shown in Figure 3. The first plait in each case
is *a* over *b*.

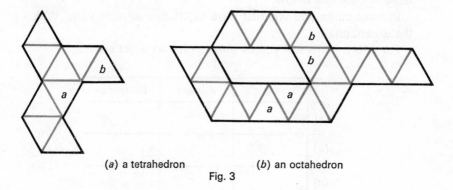

(*a*) a tetrahedron   (*b*) an octahedron

Fig. 3

Figure 4 shows another net for a cube. The black dotted lines show you
how to copy the net onto squared paper. Each face of the finished cube
is formed from four right-angled triangles (see Figure 5).

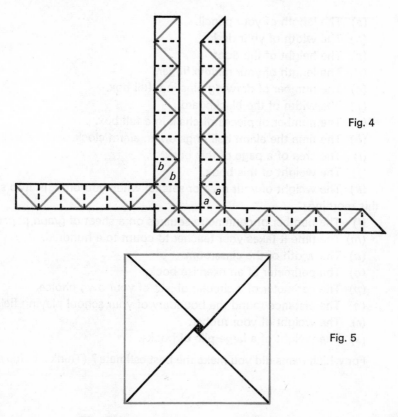

Fig. 4

Fig. 5

ESTIMATION. WHO IS THE BEST GUESSER?

Estimate and then make the measurements of items (*a*)–(*s*), completing a table like the one below.

In most cases you will first have to choose suitable units. Which are the exceptions?

For which items will you be able to give an exact answer?

	Estimation	Answer	Difference
(*a*)			
(*b*)			
(*c*)			
(*d*)			

(*a*) The length of your pencil.
(*b*) The width of your desk.
(*c*) The height of the door.
(*d*) The length of your middle finger.
(*e*) The number of drawing pins in a full box.
(*f*) The width of the blackboard.
(*g*) The number of pieces of chalk in a full box.
(*h*) The time the alarm bell rings on an alarm clock.
(*i*) The area of a page of this book.
(*j*) The weight of this book.
(*k*) The weight of your case or satchel when you brought it to school this morning.
(*l*) The number of centimetre squares on a sheet of graph paper.
(*m*) The time it takes your teacher to count to a hundred.
(*n*) The width of the classroom.
(*o*) The perimeter of an exercise book.
(*p*) The perimeter of a circular object of your own choice.
(*q*) The distance round the boundary of your school playing field.
(*r*) The weight of your rubber.
(*s*) The weight of a large pile of books.

For which items did you make the best estimate? (Think carefully.)

4. Multiplication and division of decimals

1. MULTIPLICATION AND DIVISION BY POWERS OF 10

What calculations do Figures 1 (*a*) and (*b*) show?

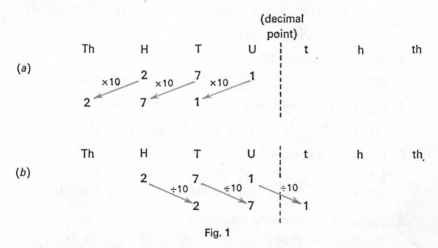

Fig. 1

Figure 1 (*a*) shows that $271 \times 10 = 2710$.
Each digit has 10 times *more than* its former place value,
and moves one place to the *left* of the decimal point.

Figure 1 (*b*) shows that $271 \div 10 = 27 \cdot 1$.
Each digit has 10 times *less than* its former place value,
and moves one place to the *right* of the decimal point.

What important part does the '0' play in 2710?
Draw similar diagrams to show (*a*) 48×100; (*b*) $48 \div 100$.

Multiplication and division of decimals

Exercise A

1 What multiplications or divisions do the following diagrams show?

(a)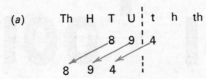

(b)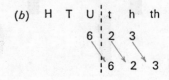

(c)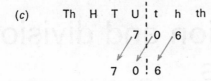

(d)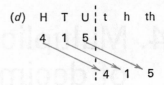

2 Write down the answer to:

(a) 332×10;   (b) 41×1000;   (c) 910×100;

(d) $4 \cdot 8 \times 100$;   (e) $50 \cdot 6 \times 10$;   (f) $0 \cdot 08 \times 10$;

(g) $670 \div 10$;   (h) $842 \div 100$;   (i) $72 \cdot 1 \div 10$;

(j) $1 \cdot 78 \div 10$;   (k) $0 \cdot 46 \div 1000$;   (l) $104 \cdot 2 \div 100$;

(m) $0 \cdot 46 \times 1000$;   (n) $56 \div 100$;   (o) $0 \cdot 003 \times 100$;

(p) $636 \div 1000$;   (q) $4 \div 10000$;   (r) $0 \cdot 082 \div 100$.

3 Write as powers of 10:

(a) 100;   (b) 1000;   (c) 10000.

4 Express in decimal form:

(a) $\frac{4}{10}$; (b) $\frac{51}{100}$; (c) $\frac{61}{1000}$; (d) $\frac{2}{100}$; (e) $\frac{21}{10}$; (f) $\frac{406}{100}$.

5 Express as a fraction:

(a) $0 \cdot 7$;   (b) $0 \cdot 89$;   (c) $0 \cdot 08$;

(d) $0 \cdot 041$;   (e) $0 \cdot 006$;   (f) $0 \cdot 0033$.

6 Complete the following equations:

(a) $93 \times ? = 9300$;   (b) $7 \cdot 48 \times ? = 74 \cdot 8$;

(c) $4800 \div ? = 480$;   (d) $0 \cdot 801 \div ? = 0 \cdot 0801$;

(e) $43 \cdot 1 \div ? = 0 \cdot 431$;   (f) $0 \cdot 076 \times ? = 76$;

(g) $0 \cdot 046 \times ? = 460$;   (h) $1 \cdot 008 \div ? = 0 \cdot 001008$;

(i) $46 \cdot 8 \times ? = 468 = ? \times 100$; (j) $0 \cdot 86 \times ? = 860 = ? \times 100$;

(k) $5100 \div ? = 511 = ? \div 100$; (l) $9 \cdot 87 \div ? = 0 \cdot 0987 = ? \div 10$.

What do you notice about your answers in parts (i) to (l)?

2. MULTIPLICATION BY MULTIPLES OF 10

How many small squares does this rectangle contain?

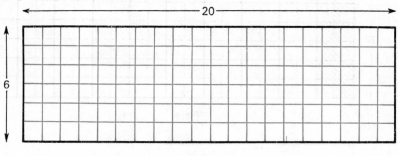

Fig. 2

You probably obtained your answer in one of three ways. What were they?

(*a*) Is it true that $6 \times 20 = 20 \times 6$?

If you take any pair of numbers and multiply them together, the order in which you write them down, makes no difference to your answer. We say that multiplication of numbers is *commutative*.

(*b*) Is it true that $20 \times 6 = 2 \times 10 \times 6 = 10 \times 2 \times 6 = 120$?

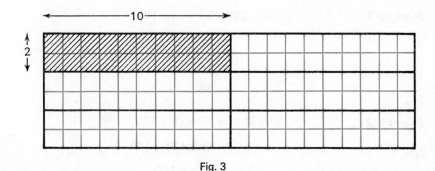

Fig. 3

Figure 3 illustrates what you will probably have noticed already; that is:

$$20 \times 6 = (2 \times 10) \times 6.$$

(*c*) What do the brackets tell you to do?

(*d*) What relations do Figures 4 and 5 show?

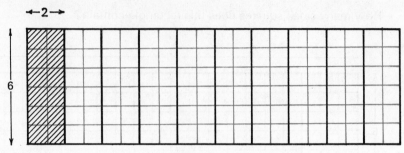

Fig. 4

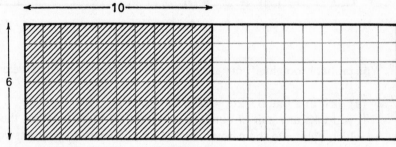

Fig. 5

We can use these ideas to help us work out products such as 34×20.

Example 1

$$34 \times 20 = 34 \times (2 \times 10)$$
$$= (34 \times 2) \times 10$$
$$= 68 \times 10$$
$$= 680.$$

Example 2

$$52 \times 800 = 52 \times (8 \times 100)$$
$$= (52 \times 8) \times 100$$
$$= 416 \times 100$$
$$= 41\,600.$$

Exercise B

1 Work out the following products. (You may find that with practice you can just write down the answer.)

(*a*) 13×20; (*b*) 42×30; (*c*) 120×400;

(*d*) 101×500; (*e*) 12×5000; (*f*) 419×20;

(g) 812×200;   (h) 141×50;   (i) 1201×40;

(j) 30×122;   (k) 200×54;   (l) 60×122.

3. MULTIPLICATION

3.1 Multiplication of any two whole numbers

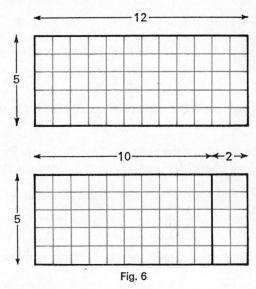

Fig. 6

Figure 6 shows that

$$5 \times 12 = 5 \times (10+2)$$
$$= (5 \times 10) + (5 \times 2)$$
$$= 50 + 10$$
$$= 60.$$

How does this working differ from that in Examples 1 and 2?

Example 3

Similarly, we could write   *or* we could set it down as

$$23 \times 36 = 23 \times (30+6)$$
$$= (23 \times 30) + (23 \times 6)$$
$$= 690 + 138$$
$$= 828$$

$$
\begin{array}{r}
23 \\
\times \quad 36 \\
\hline
690 \\
138 \\
\hline
828 \\
\hline
\end{array}
$$

Sketch a diagram like Figure 6 to illustrate the first method.

61

Example 4

$$381 \times 245 = 381 \times (200 + 40 + 5)$$

or

$$= (381 \times 200) + (381 \times 40) + (381 \times 5)$$

$$= 76\,200 + 15\,240 + 1905$$

$$= 93\,345$$

$$
\begin{array}{r}
381 \\
\times \quad 245 \\
\hline
76\,200 \\
15\,240 \\
1\,905 \\
\hline
93\,345 \\
\hline
\end{array}
$$

Multiply (*a*) 54 by 16; (*b*) 183 by 152 using both the methods just described.

3.2 Multiplication of a decimal number by a whole number

In *Book B* you found that the position of the decimal point did not alter the basic operations of addition and subtraction; for example:

(*a*)

$$
\begin{array}{r}
237 \\
+\,121 \\
\hline
358 \\
\end{array}
\qquad \text{and} \qquad
\begin{array}{r}
2\cdot37 \\
+\,1\cdot21 \\
\hline
3\cdot58 \\
\end{array}
$$

(*b*)

$$
\begin{array}{r}
563 \\
-\,211 \\
\hline
352 \\
\end{array}
\qquad \text{and} \qquad
\begin{array}{r}
56\cdot3 \\
-\,21\cdot1 \\
\hline
35\cdot2 \\
\end{array}
$$

The same is true for multiplication by a whole number. See Figure 7.

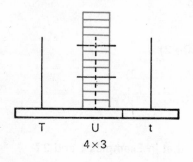

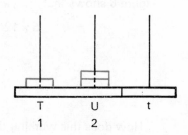

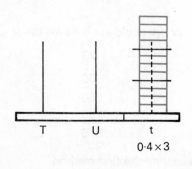

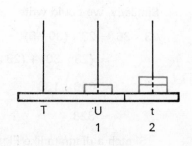

Fig. 7

What are   (a) 2×6, $0 \cdot 2 \times 6$;

                   (b) 30×7, $0 \cdot 3 \times 7$;

                   (c) 5×3, $0 \cdot 05 \times 3$?

Also, remembering that we can write

$$13 \cdot 4 \times 5 \quad \text{as} \quad (10 + 3 + 0 \cdot 4) \times 5,$$

and that multiplication is repeated addition, we have

$$13 \cdot 4 \times 5 = (10 \times 5) + (3 \times 5) + (0 \cdot 4 \times 5).$$

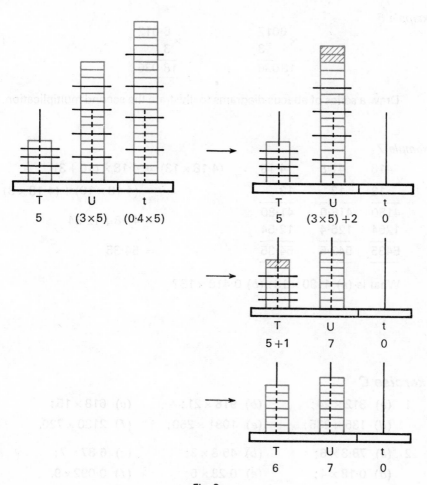

Fig. 8

Multiplication and division of decimals

Example 5

We have just shown on the abacus that $13 \cdot 4 \times 5 = 67 \cdot 0$. Notice that

$$
\begin{array}{r} 1340 \\ \times \quad 5 \\ \hline 6700 \end{array}
\qquad
\begin{array}{r} 134 \\ \times \quad 5 \\ \hline 670 \end{array}
\qquad
\begin{array}{r} 13 \cdot 4 \\ \times \quad 5 \\ \hline 67 \cdot 0 \end{array}
\qquad
\begin{array}{r} 1 \cdot 34 \\ \times \quad 5 \\ \hline 6 \cdot 70 \end{array}
\qquad
\begin{array}{r} 0 \cdot 134 \\ \times \quad 5 \\ \hline 0 \cdot 670 \end{array}
$$

What is (a) 13400×5; (b) $0 \cdot 0134 \times 5$?

Example 6

$$
\begin{array}{r} 6012 \\ \times \quad 3 \\ \hline 18036 \end{array}
\qquad\qquad
\begin{array}{r} 6 \cdot 012 \\ \times \quad 3 \\ \hline 18 \cdot 036 \end{array}
$$

Draw a series of abacus diagrams to illustrate the second multiplication.

Example 7

$$
\begin{array}{r} 418 \\ \times \quad 13 \\ \hline 4180 \\ 1254 \\ \hline 5435 \end{array}
\qquad
\begin{array}{r} 41 \cdot 8 \\ \times \quad 13 \\ \hline 418 \cdot 0 \\ 125 \cdot 4 \\ \hline 543 \cdot 5 \end{array}
\qquad
\begin{array}{r} 4 \cdot 18 \\ \times \quad 13 \\ \hline 41 \cdot 80 \\ 12 \cdot 54 \\ \hline 54 \cdot 35 \end{array}
$$

$$
\begin{aligned}
(4 \cdot 18 \times 13) &= 4 \cdot 18 \times (10 + 3) \\
&= (4 \cdot 18 \times 10) + (4 \cdot 18 \times 3) \\
&= 41 \cdot 8 + 12 \cdot 54 \\
&= 54 \cdot 35
\end{aligned}
$$

What is (a) 4180×13; (b) $0 \cdot 418 \times 13$?

Exercise C

1   (a) 312×24;   (b) 918×21;   (c) 618×15;
   (d) 135×235;   (e) 1081×260;   (f) 2130×720.

2   (a) $78 \cdot 3 \times 6$;   (b) $45 \cdot 8 \times 3$;   (c) $6 \cdot 87 \times 7$;
   (d) $0 \cdot 18 \times 4$;   (e) $0 \cdot 28 \times 6$;   (f) $0 \cdot 092 \times 9$.

3   (a) $1 \cdot 32 \times 13$;   (b) $14 \cdot 5 \times 21$;   (c) $17 \cdot 9 \times 32$;
   (d) $3 \cdot 6 \times 240$;   (e) $0 \cdot 89 \times 14$;   (f) $0 \cdot 482 \times 31$;
   (g) $0 \cdot 813 \times 520$;   (h) $0 \cdot 072 \times 28$;   (i) $0 \cdot 046 \times 97$.

3.3 Multiplication of a decimal number by a decimal number

We already know that $0·4 \times 3 = 1·2$. We could illustrate this by drawing rectangles.

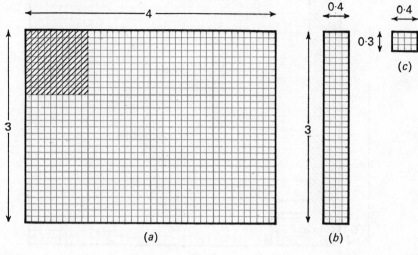

Fig. 9

What product does Figure 9 (*a*) show?
What does the shaded square represent?
By counting small squares in Figure 9 (*b*), we find that its area is

$$1\tfrac{20}{100} \text{ units} = 1·2 \text{ units.}$$

How many of these rectangles will fit into the large one?
Is this what you would have expected? Why?
The area of Figure 9 (*c*) represents $0·4 \times 0·3$. What would you expect the answer to be?

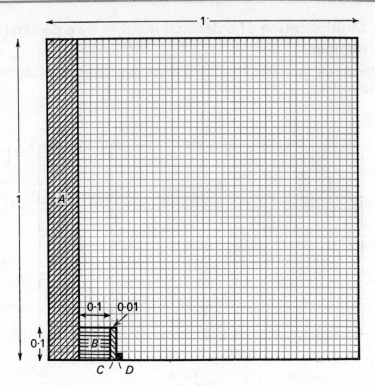

Fig. 10

In Figure 10,

the large square, *S*, represents $\qquad$ $1 \times 1 = 1$;

the rectangle, *A*, represents $\qquad$ $1 \times 0\cdot1 = 0\cdot1$;
(its area is $\frac{1}{10}$ of *S* or 0·1 of *S*)

the square, *B*, represents $\qquad$ $0\cdot1 \times 0\cdot1 = 0\cdot01$.
(its area is $\frac{1}{100}$ or 0·01 of *S*)

What do *C* and *D* represent?
These results are included in the following table. Which entries haven't we represented? How would you do so?

$1 \times 1 = 1$	$0\cdot1 \times 1 = 0\cdot1$	$0\cdot01 \times 1 = 0\cdot01$
$1 \times 0\cdot1 = 0\cdot1$	$0\cdot1 \times 0\cdot1 = 0\cdot01$	$0\cdot01 \times 0\cdot1 = 0\cdot001$
$1 \times 0\cdot01 = 0\cdot01$	$0\cdot1 \times 0\cdot01 = 0\cdot001$	$0\cdot01 \times 0\cdot01 = 0\cdot0001$

What patterns among the numbers can you see? Add another row to the table.

Notice that we could re-write the decimals in fractional form.

$$1 \times 1 \quad = 1 \qquad \frac{1}{10} \times 1 \quad = \frac{1}{10} \qquad \frac{1}{100} \times 1 \quad = \frac{1}{100}$$
$$1 \times \frac{1}{10} = \frac{1}{10} \qquad \frac{1}{10} \times \frac{1}{10} = \frac{1}{100} \qquad \frac{1}{100} \times \frac{1}{10} = \frac{1}{1000}$$
$$1 \times \frac{1}{100} = \frac{1}{100} \qquad \frac{1}{10} \times \frac{1}{100} = \frac{1}{1000} \qquad \frac{1}{100} \times \frac{1}{100} = \frac{1}{10000}$$

The rectangle, X, represents $0{\cdot}6 \times 0{\cdot}4 = 0{\cdot}24$, since its area is $\frac{24}{100}$ of the whole square.

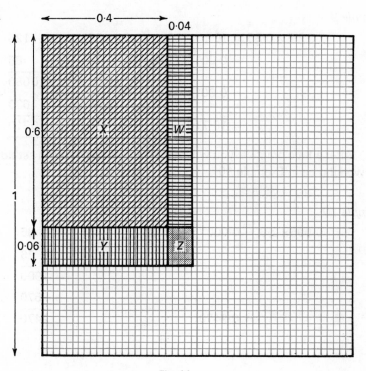

Fig. 11

What do the rectangles, W, Y, Z, represent?
We could write

$$0{\cdot}6 \times 0{\cdot}4 = (0{\cdot}1 \times 6) \times (0{\cdot}1 \times 4)$$

$$= (0{\cdot}1 \times 0{\cdot}1) \times (6 \times 4)$$

$$= 0{\cdot}01 \times 24$$

$$= 0{\cdot}24.$$

We are now able to multiply any decimal number by any other one.

Example 8

$$6\cdot8 \times 1\cdot3 = (0\cdot1 \times 68) \times (0\cdot1 \times 13)$$
$$= (0\cdot1 \times 0\cdot1) \times (68 \times 13)$$
$$= 0\cdot01 \times 884$$
$$= 8\cdot84$$

```
    68
  ×
    13
   ───
   680
   204
   ───
   884
   ───
```

Example 9

$$12\cdot6 \times 0\cdot85 = (0\cdot1 \times 126) \times (0\cdot01 \times 85)$$
$$= 0\cdot001 \times (126 \times 85)$$
$$= 0\cdot001 \times 10710$$
$$= 10\cdot710$$

```
     126
   ×
      85
   ─────
   10080
     630
   ─────
   10710
   ─────
```

After a little practice, you will probably find that you can set down your working as in Example 10.

Example 10

$$0\cdot095 \times 2\cdot6 = 0\cdot0001 \times 95 \times 26$$

$$= 0\cdot2470$$

```
    95
  ×
    26
  ────
  1900
   570
  ────
  2470
  ────
```

Exercise D

Work out the following products. (You may find that you can just write down the answers.)

1. (a) $0\cdot02 \times 0\cdot03$; (b) $0\cdot02 \times 0\cdot003$; (c) $0\cdot006 \times 0\cdot02$;
   (d) $1\cdot02 \times 0\cdot7$; (e) $7\cdot5 \times 0\cdot02$; (f) $1\cdot2 \times 0\cdot012$;
   (g) $40 \times 0\cdot02$; (h) $70 \times 0\cdot04$; (i) $600 \times 0\cdot09$.

2. (a) $27 \times 9\cdot5$; (b) $45 \times 0\cdot32$; (c) $360 \times 0\cdot82$;
   (d) $6\cdot2 \times 7\cdot7$; (e) $5\cdot5 \times 8\cdot1$; (f) $2\cdot6 \times 9\cdot5$;
   (g) $0\cdot75 \times 4\cdot8$; (h) $0\cdot51 \times 0\cdot62$; (i) $0\cdot73 \times 0\cdot84$;

(*j*) $24 \cdot 1 \times 3 \cdot 5$;   (*k*) $4 \cdot 3 \times 0 \cdot 087$;   (*l*) $0 \cdot 803 \times 0 \cdot 61$;

(*m*) $0 \cdot 062 \times 0 \cdot 43$;   (*n*) $28 \cdot 7 \times 9 \cdot 03$;   (*o*) $23 \cdot 42 \times 10 \cdot 1$;

(*p*) $210 \cdot 8 \times 0 \cdot 0052$; (*q*) $200 \cdot 5 \times 0 \cdot 051$;   (*r*) $30 \cdot 08 \times 0 \cdot 765$.

4. DIVISION

4.1 Division and repeated subtraction

We can write $7 + 7 + 7 + 7 + 7 + 7 + 7 + 7 + 7 = 7 \times 9 = 63$.

(*a*) What is $63 - 7 - 7 - 7 - 7 - 7 - 7 - 7 - 7 - 7$?

(*b*) What is $63 \div 7$?

(*c*) Explain the connection between the last two questions.

(*d*) If you were to work out $65 - 7 - 7 - 7 - 7 - 7 - 7 - 7 - 7 - 7$, what would you find? How would you give your answer?

4.2 Division of a whole number by a whole number

Example 11 (*Method I*)

If you were asked to work out $5489 \div 12$ by finding out how many times you could subtract 12 from 5489, you wouldn't be very pleased!

$$
\begin{array}{r}
5489 \\
- 12 \\
\hline
5477 \\
- 12 \\
\hline
5465 \\
- 12 \\
\hline
5453 \\
- 12 \\
\hline
5441 \\
- 12 \\
\hline
5429 \\
- 12 \\
\hline
5417 \\
\vdots
\end{array}
$$

This is just the start. It would certainly take a long time. However, as you will have realized, there are quicker ways of doing this division.

Multiplication and division of decimals

(*Method II*)

12)5489

  4800 (400 twelves)
   689

   600 (50 twelves)
    89

    84 (7 twelves)
     5

Consider 5400. There are more than 400 (but less than 500) twelves in 5400. Let us subtract 400 of them all at once.

Now consider 680. There are more than 50 (but less than 60) twelves in 680. Subtract 50 of these all at once.

Finally, we know that there are 7 twelves in 89 which if we subtract them leave us with a remainder of 5.

So we have subtracted $(400 + 50 + 7)$ twelves and have 5 left over.

$$5489 \div 12 = 457, \quad \text{remainder } 5.$$

If we were dividing in order to find the answer to a 'fair shares' question, we would write $\qquad 5489 \div 12 = 457\frac{5}{12}.$

You will probably have recognized this method. Why?

(*Method III*)

$$\begin{array}{r} 457 \\ 12\overline{)5489} \\ 4800 \\ \hline 680 \\ 600 \\ \hline 89 \\ 84 \\ \hline 5 \end{array}$$

Method III shows you that Method II is equivalent to the ordinary method of long division. Notice that we usually leave out the dotted zeros.

Example 12

Calculate $6318 \div 22$

$$\begin{array}{r} 287 \\ 22\overline{)6318} \\ 44 \\ \hline 191 \\ 176 \\ \hline 158 \\ 154 \\ \hline 4 \end{array}$$

The answer is 287, remainder 4, or $287\frac{4}{22}$.

Explain exactly what you are doing at each stage of this division.

4.3 Division of a decimal number by a whole number

Example 13

Calculate : (*a*) $8364 \div 34$; (*b*) $83 \cdot 64 \div 34$.

(*a*)	246		(*b*)	2·46	
34)8364				34)83·64	
	68	(200 34's)		68	(2 34's)
	156			15·6	
	136	(40 34's)		13·6	(0·4 34's)
	204			2·04	
	204	(6 34's)		2·04	(0·06 34's)

So,

$$8364 \div 34 = 246 \quad \text{and} \quad 83 \cdot 64 \div 34 = 2 \cdot 46.$$

What is the answer to

(i) $83\,640 \div 34$,   (ii) $8 \cdot 364 \div 34$,   (iii) $0 \cdot 8364 \div 34$?

Exercise E

In Questions 1–8, work out (*a*) by long division, and then *write down* the answers to (*b*) and (*c*).

1   (*a*) $4095 \div 13$;   (*b*) $409 \cdot 5 \div 13$;   (*c*) $40\,950 \div 13$.

2   (*a*) $3189 \div 24$;   (*b*) $318\,900 \div 24$;   (*c*) $31 \cdot 89 \div 24$.

3   (*a*) $6764 \div 76$;   (*b*) $67 \cdot 64 \div 76$;   (*c*) $0 \cdot 6764 \div 76$.

4   (*a*) $88\,326 \div 42$;   (*b*) $88\,326 \div 420$;   (*c*) $88 \cdot 326 \div 42$.

5   (*a*) $91 \cdot 35 \div 63$;   (*b*) $91\,350 \div 63$;   (*c*) $91 \cdot 35 \div 6 \cdot 3$.

6   (*a*) $2073 \cdot 5 \div 29$;   (*b*) $2073 \cdot 5 \div 0 \cdot 29$;   (*c*) $2073 \cdot 5 \div 2900$.

7   (*a*) $86 \cdot 8 \div 31$;   (*b*) $0 \cdot 868 \div 31$;   (*c*) $86 \cdot 8 \div 3 \cdot 1$.

8   (*a*) $41 \cdot 87 \div 53$;   (*b*) $4 \cdot 187 \div 5 \cdot 3$;   (*c*) $4187 \div 530$.

9   Calculate :

(*a*) $91 \cdot 63 \div 17$;   (*b*) $8 \cdot 61 \div 21$;   (*c*) $7 \cdot 776 \div 36$;

(*d*) $28 \cdot 272 \div 57$;   (*e*) $0 \cdot 75 \div 15$;   (*f*) $0 \cdot 864 \div 24$;

(*g*) $0 \cdot 0936 \div 36$;   (*h*) $82 \cdot 4 \div 206$;   (*i*) $4 \cdot 2 \div 28$;

(*j*) $48 \div 320$;   (*k*) $0 \cdot 84 \div 24$;   (*l*) $0 \cdot 084 \div 24$.

10   2700 m of wire has to be divided into 36 equal lengths. How long will each piece be?

11 7500 bars of chocolate have to be packed into boxes containing 48 bars each. How many boxes will be filled and how many bars of chocolate will be left over?

12 £320·76 has been collected and is to be shared equally between 18 charities. How much will each one receive?

4.4 Division of a decimal number by a decimal number

Try to divide 319·5 by 0·15. Is it immediately obvious where to put the digits of the answer in relation to the decimal point?

We can write $319·5 \div 0·15$ in fraction form as $\dfrac{319·5}{0·15}$.

We could choose to write this as

$$\frac{319·5 \times 10}{0·15 \times 10} = \frac{3195}{1·5} = 3195 \div 1·5,$$

or

$$\frac{319·5 \times 100}{0·15 \times 100} = \frac{31\,950}{15} = 31\,950 \div 15,$$

or

$$\frac{319·5 \times 1000}{0·15 \times 1000} = \frac{319\,500}{150} = 319\,500 \div 150.$$

Which of the three divisions would you find the easiest to do? Why? Now do it. What is the answer to $319·5 \div 0·15$?

Example 14

Calculate $38·16 \div 1·8$.

$$38·16 \div 1·8 = \frac{38·16}{1·8} = \frac{38·16 \times 10}{1·8 \,\times 10} = \frac{381·6}{18} = 381·6 \div 18.$$

$$
\begin{array}{r}
21·2 \\
18\overline{)381·6} \\
36 \\
\hline
21 \\
18 \\
\hline
3·6 \\
3·6 \\
\hline
\end{array}
$$

So $38·16 \div 1·8 = 21·2$.

What is:

(i) $3816 \div 1·8$,   (ii) $38·16 \div 180$?

(*a*) Calculate $58 \cdot 65 \div 0 \cdot 51$, noticing that

$$58 \cdot 65 \div 0 \cdot 51 = \frac{58 \cdot 65}{0 \cdot 51} = \frac{58 \cdot 65 \times 100}{0 \cdot 51 \times 100} = \frac{5865}{51} = 5865 \div 51.$$

What is:

       (i) $58 \cdot 65 \div 0 \cdot 051$,   (ii) $58 \cdot 65 \div 510$?

(*b*) Calculate $9 \cdot 425 \div 0 \cdot 065$ noticing that

$$9 \cdot 425 \div 0 \cdot 065 = \frac{9 \cdot 425}{0 \cdot 065} = \frac{9 \cdot 425 \times 1000}{0 \cdot 065 \times 1000} = \frac{9425}{65} = 9425 \div 65.$$

What is:

       (i) $9 \cdot 425 \div 6 \cdot 5$,   (ii) $94 \cdot 25 \div 0 \cdot 65$?

Exercise F

1 If $28\,272 \div 57 = 496$, write down the answers to the following:

    (*a*) $282 \cdot 72 \div 57$;   (*b*) $28\,272 \div 5700$;   (*c*) $28\,272 \div 0 \cdot 57$;

    (*d*) $28\,272 \div 0 \cdot 057$;   (*e*) $282 \cdot 72 \div 0 \cdot 57$;   (*f*) $282\,720 \div 0 \cdot 57$.

2 Calculate:

    (*a*) $868 \div 0 \cdot 2$;   (*b*) $0 \cdot 432 \div 0 \cdot 3$;   (*c*) $81 \cdot 2 \div 0 \cdot 4$;

    (*d*) $5 \cdot 35 \div 0 \cdot 05$;   (*e*) $12 \cdot 88 \div 0 \cdot 07$;   (*f*) $9 \cdot 812 \div 1 \cdot 1$;

    (*g*) $252 \div 0 \cdot 12$;   (*h*) $353 \cdot 1 \div 0 \cdot 11$;   (*i*) $0 \cdot 5278 \div 0 \cdot 13$;

    (*j*) $418 \cdot 2 \div 0 \cdot 34$;   (*k*) $34 \cdot 72 \div 3 \cdot 1$;   (*l*) $9 \cdot 022 \div 0 \cdot 026$;

    (*m*) $19 \cdot 228 \div 0 \cdot 44$; (*n*) $7 \cdot 296 \div 0 \cdot 48$;   (*o*) $0 \cdot 7385 \div 3 \cdot 5$;

    (*p*) $2051 \cdot 3 \div 0 \cdot 073$; (*q*) $3962 \cdot 7 \div 1 \cdot 11$;   (*r*) $12816 \div 14 \cdot 4$.

3 Calculate answers to the following correct to 2 significant figures:

    (*a*) $54 \div 1 \cdot 2$;   (*b*) $98 \div 3 \cdot 5$;   (*c*) $850 \div 0 \cdot 34$;

    (*d*) $0 \cdot 99 \div 5 \cdot 4$;   (*e*) $0 \cdot 91 \div 0 \cdot 24$;   (*f*) $46 \div 0 \cdot 38$;

    (*g*) $930 \div 1 \cdot 6$;   (*h*) $7 \cdot 3 \div 0 \cdot 017$;   (*i*) $76 \div 0 \cdot 019$.

Miscellaneous Exercise G

1 A footballer in training runs 800 m every day. How many km is this per week?

2 If I earn £11·85 per week, how much is this per year?

Multiplication and division of decimals

3 If I have £3 to spend on records, how many costing £0·35 each can I buy?

4 A man buys 2 kg of apples at £0·15 per kg and 1·5 kg of pears at £0·18 per kg. How much change would he receive from a £1 note?

5 A square has side 0·04 m. What is its area (a) in m²; (b) in cm²?

6 Find the cost of 4·45 litres of petrol at 3·9 francs per litre.

7 How many test tubes containing 32 cm³ of liquid could be *filled* from a beaker holding 3 litres? (1 litre = 1000 cm³.)

8 A box weighs 0·95 kg and contains bars of chocolate weighing 0·12 kg each. How much will the box together with the bars of chocolate weigh if there are (a) 8, (b) 65 bars in the box? How many bars are there in the box when the total weight is (c) 2·35 kg, (d) 5·99 kg?

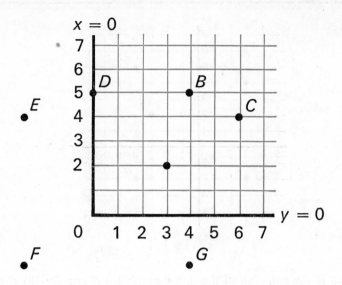

5. Extending graphs

1. POINTS AND LINES

In the diagram at the head of this chapter, A is the point (3, 2).

What are the coordinates of B, C and D?

Can you suggest a way in which the positions of E, F and G could also be described?

We have already used the set of directed numbers to name points on the number line to the left and right of 0. If we now draw a second number line at right-angles to the first, we can name all the points in the plane.

Look at Figure 1 (overleaf). Since the x-coordinate of a point is taken from the set of numbers across the page, E's x-coordinate is ⁻3. The y-coordinate comes from the set of numbers up the page, so E's y-co-ordinate is ⁺4 and E is the point (⁻3, ⁺4).

Write down the coordinates of A, B, C, D, F and G.

What can you say about the y-coordinates of C and E? Are there any other points with the same y-coordinate? What is the equation of the line through C and E?

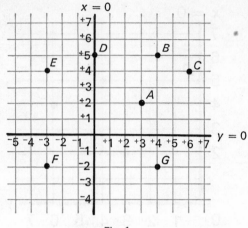

Fig. 1

What is the equation of the line through (*a*) *B* and *D*; (*b*) *B* and *G*; (*c*) *E* and *F*; (*d*) *F* and *G*?

Exercise A

1

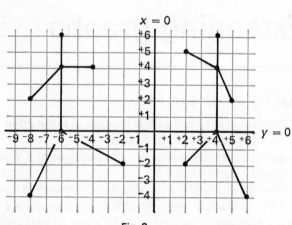

Fig. 2

Figure 2 shows two pin-men. What are the coordinates of the points marked in black?

2 On a grid like that in Figure 2, plot the points with coordinates: (0, +3), (+6, +1), (+6, 0), (0, 0), (0, −4), (+2, −5), (+2, −6), (−3, −6), (−3, −5), (−1, −4), (−1, 0), (−7, 0), (−7, +1), (−1, +3), (−1, +5), (−$\frac{1}{2}$, +6), (0, +5). Join them up in the order in which they are written. What picture do you get?

3   On a grid like that in Figure 2, draw a picture of your own which can easily be described by the coordinates of its corners. Read out the coordinates to your neighbour. See if he or she can plot them correctly and discover what you have drawn.

4   Plot on squared paper the points A ($^-3$, 0), B ($^-1$, $^+3$), C ($^+1$, 0) and D ($^-1$, $^-6$).

(*a*) What kind of quadrilateral is *ABCD*?

(*b*) Write down the equation of:

(i) the line through A and C;

(ii) the line through B and D.

(*c*) Find the area of the quadrilateral.

5   Plot on squared paper the points P (0, $^-3$), Q ($^-2$, 0) and R ($^+1$, $^+2$). P, Q and R are three vertices of the square *PQRS*. Mark the point S on your diagram.

(*a*) What are the coordinates of S?

(*b*) What are the coordinates of the centre of the square?

6   Plot on squared paper the points with coordinates: ($^-5$, $^-4$), ($^-3$, $^-2$), ($^-1$, 0), ($^+1$, $^+2$), ($^+3$, $^+4$). What do you notice? Suggest a relation which is satisfied by the x- and y-coordinates of these five points.

7   Plot on squared paper the points with coordinates:

($^-5$, $^+7$), ($^-3$, $^+5$), ($^-1$, $^+3$), ($^+1$, $^+1$), ($^+2$, 0), ($^+4$, $^-2$), ($^+6$, $^-4$).

What do you notice? Suggest a relation which is satisfied by the x- and y-coordinates of these seven points.

8   W ($^-2$, 0), X ($^+1$, $^+3$) and Y ($^+2$, $^+2$) are three vertices of the rectangle *WXYZ*.

(*a*) State the coordinates of Z.

(*b*) Write down the coordinates of four points on the line through W and X.

What is the equation of this line?

(*c*) What is the equation of the line through:

(i) X and Y;   (ii) Y and Z;   (iii) Z and W?

9

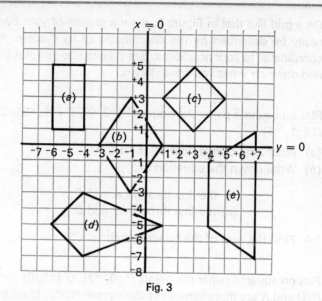

Fig. 3

For each of the quadrilaterals shown in Figure 3, state:

(i)   its special name;

(ii) the coordinates of its vertices;

(iii) the equation(s) of its line(s) of symmetry.

2. REGIONS

(a)

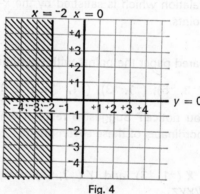

Fig. 4

Look at Figure 4. The plane is divided into two regions by the line $x = {}^-2$. Write down the coordinates of some points in the shaded region. Does it matter what numbers you choose for their x-coordinates? Does it matter what numbers you choose for their y-coordinates? How would you describe the shaded region? Is this the region $x < {}^-2$ or $x > {}^-2$? How would you describe the unshaded region?

(*b*) On a diagram mark the line $y = ^-1$. Shade the region $y > ^-1$. How would you describe the unshaded region?

Exercise B

1   Describe the shaded regions in Figure 5.

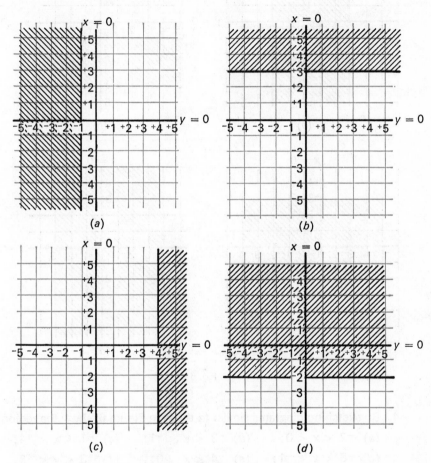

(*a*)

(*b*)

(*c*)

(*d*)

Fig. 5

2   By sketching diagrams similar to those in Figure 5, show the regions:

(*a*) $x > ^+3$;   (*b*) $y > ^+1$;   (*c*) $x < ^+4$;

(*d*) $y < ^-2$;   (*e*) $y > ^-3$;   (*f*) $y < ^+3$;

(*g*) $x < ^-4$;   (*h*) $x > 0$;   (*i*) $y < 0$;

(*j*) $^+1 < x$;   (*k*) $^-3 > y$;   (*l*) $^+2 > y$.

3. Describe the shaded regions in Figure 6.

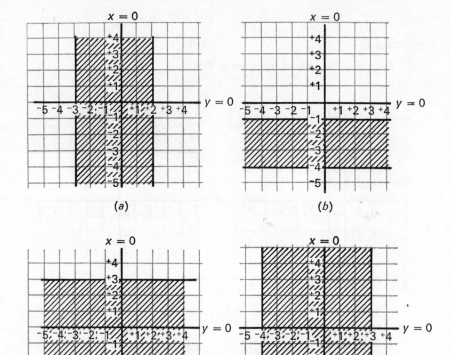

(a)

(b)

(c)

(d)

Fig. 6

4 By sketching diagrams similar to those in Figure 6, show the regions:

(a) $^-2 < x < 0$; (b) $^-3 < y < ^-1$; (c) $^-1 < x < ^+4$;

(d) $^-5 < x < ^-1$; (e) $^-4 < x < 0$; (f) $^-3 < y < ^+3$;

(g) $^-1 < y < ^+2$; (h) $^+3 > x > ^+1$; (i) $0 > y > ^-2$.

5 Let p be the region $x < ^+2$ and q be the region $y > ^-1$. On a diagram, show p by horizontal shading and q by vertical shading. Colour the region $p \cap q$.

6 Let r be the region $x < ^-3$ and s be the region $y < 0$. On a diagram, show by different shadings, the regions r and s. Colour the region $r \cap s$.

7 Let t be the region $^+1 < x < ^+3$ and u be the region $^-4 < y < ^-1$. Show by shading the region $t \cap u$.

8 Let v be the region $^-4 < x < 0$ and w be the region $^-1 < y < ^+2$. Show by shading the region $v \cap w$.

9

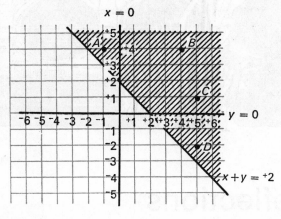

Fig. 7

In Figure 7, the line $x + y = ^+2$ divides the plane into two regions. How many sets of points are there?

(a) Write down the coordinates of A, B, C and D. Find the sum of the coordinates, that is the value of $x + y$, for each of these four points.

(b) Write down the coordinates of some other points which lie *above* the line in the shaded region. Is it always true that $x + y > ^+2$?

(c) Write down the coordinates of some points *below* the line in the unshaded region. What can you say about the value of $x + y$? How would you describe the unshaded region?

10 Draw the line $y = x + ^+1$. This line divides the plane into two regions. Mark some points in each of these regions and by examining the coordinates of the marked points, find a way of describing the regions. Label the regions clearly.

11 By sketching diagrams similar to that in Figure 7, show the regions:

(a) $x + y > ^-2$;   (b) $x + y < ^-1$;   (c) $y > x$;

(d) $y < x + ^+3$;   (e) $y > x + ^-2$;   (f) $y < x - ^+1$.

6. Reflections

1. OBJECTS AND IMAGES

(a) (i) When we say that Figure 1 has line symmetry, what do we mean?

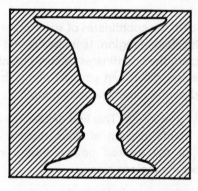

Fig. 1

(ii) Here is a way of checking for line symmetry. Put the edge of a mirror onto the suspected line of symmetry. Is the shape you can see in the mirror exactly like the shape behind the mirror? Can you see the original picture, half on the paper and half in the mirror? If you can, you have found the line of symmetry.

Put a mirror on the red lines in Figure 2. Look at the reflections and see if the shape has appeared to change. Which of the red lines are lines of symmetry?

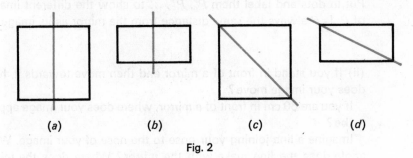

(a)   (b)   (c)   (d)

Fig. 2

Repeat the experiment with the diagrams of Figure 3.

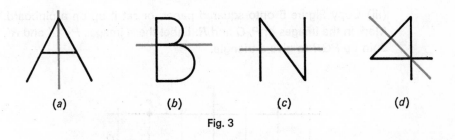

(a)   (b)   (c)   (d)

Fig. 3

(b) (i) Copy Figure 4 onto squared paper. Put the edge of a mirror on the line *m*. Hold it at right-angles to the page. Look at the reflection of *P*. Where does it appear to be on the grid?

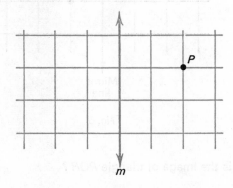

Fig. 4

Remove the mirror and make a dot for the reflection of *P*. Label this dot *P'* (pronounced '*P* dash'). *P* is called the *object* and *P'* is its *image*. We say that *P maps* onto *P'*.

Move the mirror to different positions but always parallel to *m*. Put in dots and label them *P"*, *P'''*, ... to show the different images of *P*. Is *P* always the same distance from the mirror as its image?

(ii) If you stand in front of a mirror and then move towards it, how does your image move?

If you are 60 cm in front of a mirror, where does your image appear to be?

Imagine a line joining your nose to the nose of your image. What angle does the line make with the mirror? Where does the mirror cut the line?

(iii) Copy Figure 5 onto squared paper, or set it up on a pinboard. Mark in the images of *P*, *Q* and *R*. Label these images *P'*, *Q'* and *R'*. Join up *PQR* to give a triangle.

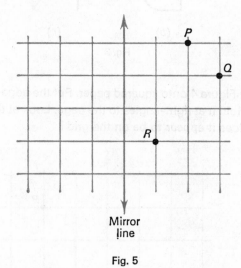

Mirror
line

Fig. 5

What is the image of triangle *PQR*?

(iv) Copy Figure 6 onto squared paper or use a pinboard, and put in the images.

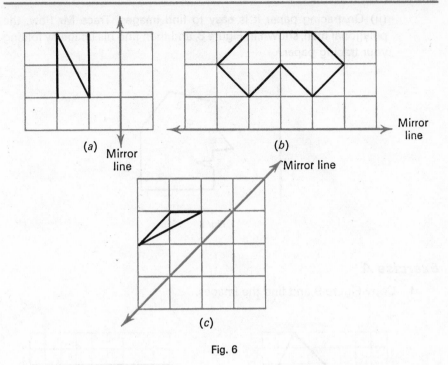

Fig. 6

(*c*) (i) It is easier to draw images on squared paper because of the grid of lines. It is more difficult on plain paper: one method is to fold the paper on the mirror line so that the object is on the outside, and then dot through with a pencil or prick with a pin or compass point.

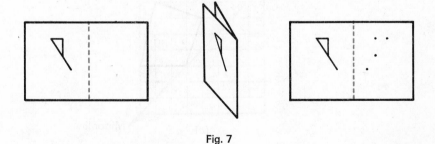

Fig. 7

Draw an object and a mirror line on a sheet of paper. By folding and pricking through, find the image (see Figure 7).

(ii) On tracing paper it is easy to find images. Trace Mr Poly, the polygonal man, shown in Figure 8, and then find his image by folding your tracing paper.

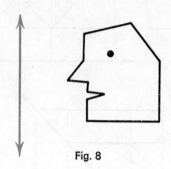

Fig. 8

Exercise A

1   Copy Figure 9 and find the images.

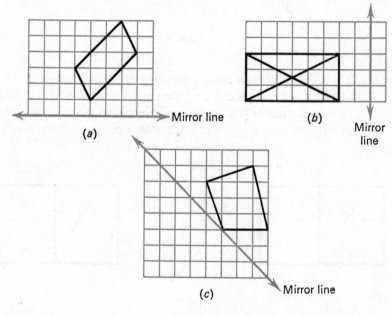

Fig. 9

2   Trace Figure 10 and find the image on your tracing paper.

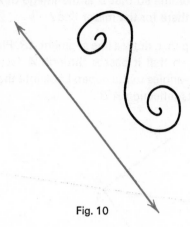

Fig. 10

3   Copy Figure 11 and put in the images *freehand* (without folding your paper or using tracing paper).

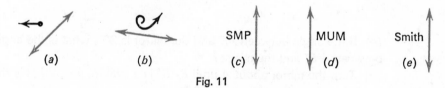

(a)   (b)   (c)   SMP   (d)   MUM   (e)   Smith

Fig. 11

4   Draw objects and mirror lines. Exchange with your neighbour and put in the images. Do not make the objects too complicated.

5   Repeat Question 4, but draw the images at the same time as your partner draws the objects.

6   Draw on squared paper the lines with equations $x = 0$ and $y = 0$ so as to divide the page into four approximately equal parts.

(a) If a mirror is standing on the line $x = 0$ where would the reflection of the following points appear to be?

   (i) $(^+3, 0)$,   (ii) $(^+2, {}^+4)$,   (iii) $(^+1, {}^-3)$,
   (iv) $(0, {}^+2{\cdot}5)$,   (v) $(^+1{\cdot}5, {}^+0{\cdot}5)$.

(b)   Draw line segments joining each point to its reflection. What can you say about these line segments and the line $x = 0$?

7   If a mirror is standing on the diagonal line which passes through $(0, 0)$ and $(^+2, {}^+2)$, where would the reflection of the following points appear to be?

   (a) $(0, {}^+4)$;   (b) $(^-2, {}^-1)$;   (c) $(^+5, {}^+5)$.

8   Mark two points *A* and *B* on a sheet of tracing paper. Fold the paper to find a mirror line so that *B* is the image of *A*. How many possible positions are there for the mirror line?

9   On a sheet of paper, draw a line segment *AB*. Place the edge of a mirror on the paper so that it passes through *A* (see Figure 12). Keep the mirror at right-angles to the paper. Look into the mirror and you should see *AB* and its reflection *A'B'*.

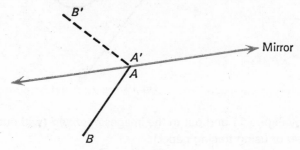

Fig. 12

(*a*) If the angle between *AB* and the mirror is 30°, what is the angle between *A'B'* and the mirror?
(*b*) Turn the mirror about *A* until *BAB'* is a straight line. What is the angle between the mirror and *AB*?

10 Draw two straight lines *p* and *q* (see Figure 13). Stand a mirror at their point of intersection. Look into the mirror and you should see part of the lines *p* and *q* and their reflections. Turn the mirror until the reflections are in line with *p* and *q*. Draw in the position of the mirror line when this occurs.

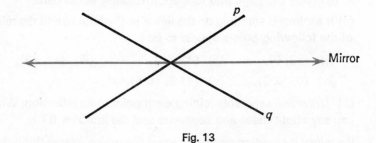

Fig. 13

(*a*) What do you notice about the position of the mirror line?
(*b*) Is there more than one possible position of the mirror line?

Summary

In a reflection, the point P maps onto the point P' such that:
  (i)   the line PP' is at right-angles to the mirror line, and
  (ii) the distance PN is the same as the distance $P'N$ (see Figure 14).

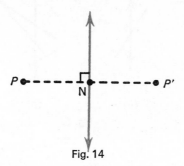

Fig. 14

2. MATHEMATICAL REFLECTIONS

Reflection in a real mirror only works from one side. If you stand behind a mirror you will not produce an image.

Now we are going to invent a mathematical mirror which is double-sided and reflects both ways! (Figure 15.)

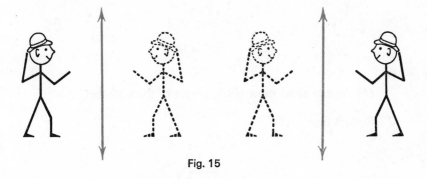

Fig. 15

Not only does P reflect to P', but also P' reflects to P in Figure 16.

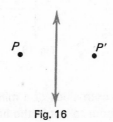

Fig. 16

Trace Figure 17 and put in the reflections. Remember these mirrors reflect both ways.

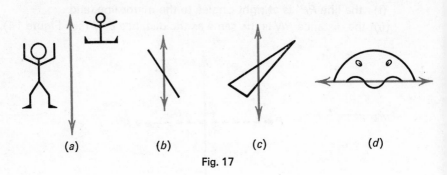

(a)   (b)   (c)   (d)

Fig. 17

Exercise B

1 (a) Copy Figure 18 and find the reflections.

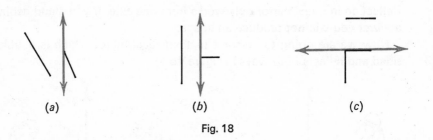

(a)   (b)   (c)

Fig. 18

(b) Invent some more using letters of the alphabet.

2 Reflect Figure 19.

Fig. 19

3 Draw an object on both sides of a mirror line as in the last question and get your neighbour to put in the image.

4 The line with equation $x = {}^+3$ is taken as the mirror line. Find the coordinates of the image of the triangle whose vertices are $(^-1, {}^-1)$, $(^+4, {}^+4)$ and $(^+3, {}^-3)$.

Draw a quadrilateral and find its reflection in the line $x = {}^+3$.

5 When an object is reflected, are any points left unchanged? Are any lines left unchanged?

6 A line of an object is at 24° to the mirror line. What can you say about the angle between its image line and the mirror? Draw a diagram to illustrate your answer.

7 The angle between an object line and its corresponding image line is 60°. Describe the position of the mirror line.

8 Fred the mathematical fly walks round the circle in Figure 20 in a clockwise direction.

Draw the path of his image in the mirror and indicate its direction.

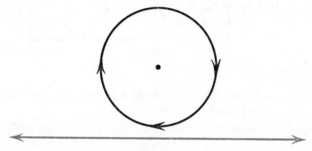

Fig. 20

9 Put a mirror on the line *m*. When you look at the reflection of the words, you can only read the one that is dotted. A possible explanation is that mirrors only reflect writing that is dotted. Do you agree with this theory?

A CHOICE REFLECTION

Repeat with CHOCK ICE, I COOK COD. Invent some more of your own.

10 A mirror image is always the same size and shape as the object. What is *different* about the object and image?

3. INVESTIGATIONS

Investigation 1

You have often looked in a mirror and studied your reflection—but have you realized that you are not seeing yourself as others see you? For example, if you wink with your right eye, which eye of your reflection appears to wink?

Hold your right hand up, like a Red Indian saying 'How'. Which hand does your image hold up?

If a mirror swaps you round right to left, left to right, why doesn't it swap you round top to bottom, bottom to top?

You can turn yourself upside down with two mirrors at right-angles (see Figure 21). Try it and see.

Fig. 21

Investigation 2

(*a*) Compare a pair of gloves. Hold a right hand glove up to a mirror. What does it look like?

Write down three other examples of things which are reflections of each other.

(*b*) The die in Figure 22 is a clockwise die. Can you see why? How would you draw its reflection?

Try to find actual examples of both of these types of die.

Fig. 22

Investigation 3

(*a*) *Challenge problem!*

You are told that in Figure 23 (opposite), *P'* is the reflection of *P*. You are not allowed to fold, use tracing paper or measure. All you may do is use a pencil and a straight edge (like a ruler with no markings on it). Find the image of *Q*.

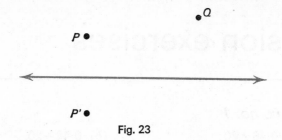

Fig. 23

(*b*) A small boat has to travel from ship *A* to ship *B* both of which are anchored near to a quay, and the journey has to be made via the quay in order to put someone down there. A possible route, for example, is *ACB* (see Figure 24).

Find the shortest route.

(*Hint:* this has something to do with (*a*).)

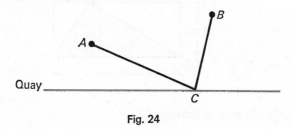

Fig. 24

(*c*) *How to play billiards by reflection!*

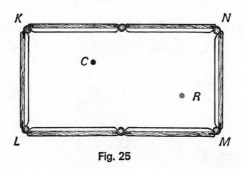

Fig. 25

Figure 25 shows the plan of a billiard table. The cue ball *C* has to be hit so that it rebounds from the cushion *LM* and strikes the red ball *R*. In which direction should it be hit? Now try to bounce it off *KN*. Can it be done off the other sides too?

Revision exercises

Quick quiz, no. 1

1 (a) $0{\cdot}48 \times 20$;   (b) $0{\cdot}48 \div 20$.

2 Convert the following into decimal numbers:
   (a) 1101_{two};   (b) 161_{eight}.

3 What is the difference in grammes between 3·4 kg and 3·2 kg?

4

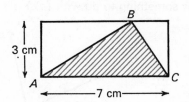

What is the area of triangle ABC?

5 What linear relation do these points satisfy?

$$(0, 7), \quad (1, 8), \quad (2, 9), \quad (3, 10).$$

6 Arrange the following numbers in order of size, smallest first.

$$^{+}1, \quad ^{-}3, \quad 0, \quad ^{-}5, \quad ^{-}2, \quad ^{+}2, \quad ^{-}1, \quad ^{+}4.$$

Quick quiz, no. 2

1 The length of a line segment is 23 cm. What is its length:
   (a) in mm;   (b) in m?

2 Write down the value of:
   (a) $0{\cdot}4 \times 0{\cdot}4$;   (b) $0{\cdot}08 \div 0{\cdot}004$.

3 A line joins $(^{-}2, {}^{+}4)$ to $(^{-}2, {}^{-}2)$. What is its equation?

4

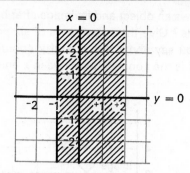

Describe the shaded region.

5 Find 3 different numbers which could be put in each of the boxes:

   (a) □ < $^+8$;   □ > $^-3$.

6 A mirror is standing on the line $x = 0$. Where would the reflection of the following appear to be?

   (a) $(^+1, ^+3)$;   (b) $(^-2, ^+4)$.

Exercise A

1 How much would it cost to carpet a room measuring 11 m by 18 m if the carpet costs £1·50 per square metre?

2 On the same diagram, draw the graph of the relations $x = 3y$ and $x = 3 + y$. Where do the lines meet?

3 Trace the pentagon in Figure 1 and find its area.

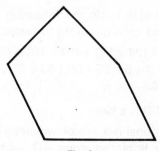

Fig. 1

4 State whether the following are true or false.

   (a) $1041 \times 108 = 108 \times 1041$;

   (b) $40 \div 80 = 80 \div 40$;

   (c) $206 \times 105 = (206 \times 100) + (206 \times 5)$;

   (d) $12 \times 5 \times 7 = 35 \times 12$.

95

5 Figure 2 shows an object and its image after being reflected. Where is the mirror line? Give the coordinates of six points on the mirror line. What can you say about the x- and y-coordinates of each of these points. What is the connection between x and y?

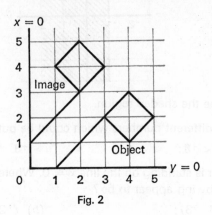

Fig. 2

Exercise B

1 Find two different numbers which can be put in each box if:

(a) $^+3 < \square < ^+8$;　　　　(b) $^-6 < \square < ^-2$;

(c) $^-3 < \square < 0$;　　　　(d) $^+5 < \square < ^+7$;

(e) $^-1 < \square < ^+2$;　　　　(f) $^-3 < \square < ^-1$.

2 On separate diagrams show, by shading, the regions:

(a) $0 < x < ^+2$;　　(b) $^-5 < y < ^-1$;　　(c) $x+y > ^+4$.

3 You should be able to do the following calculations in your head. Explain how and write down the answers.

(a) $(24 \times 70) + (24 \times 12) + (24 \times 10) + (24 \times 8)$;
(b) $1+2+3+4+5+95+96+97+98+99$;
(c) $72 \times 25 \times 4$.

4 The figure ABCD is a kite.

(a) Which diagonal is a line of symmetry?
(b) If a mirror is placed along AC, what line segment is the reflection of BC?
(c) If AC = 50 cm and BD = 30 cm, what is the area of the kite?

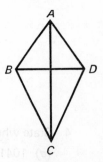

Fig. 3

5 A shopkeeper pays £362·5 for 250 dresses. If he then sells every dress for £2·95, how much profit does he make on each dress?

7. Networks

1. MATRICES FROM DRAWINGS

Figure 1 shows the network of A-roads linking some towns in Devon and Cornwall.

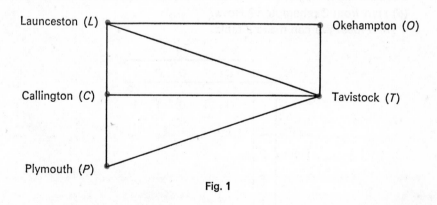

Fig. 1

(*a*) A direct route is a journey which does not pass through another town on the way. Is there a direct route from (i) *C* to *L*; (ii) *C* to *O*; no (iii) *C* to *C*? How many direct routes go to Tavistock? How many start at Launceston? 3

(*b*) One way of describing the direct routes linking the towns is to draw the map in Figure 1. Can you suggest any other ways?

First idea. We can make a list. Copy and complete Figure 2, the list of direct routes:

From	To
Callington	Launceston
Launceston	Callington
Callington	Plymouth
...	...

Fig. 2

How many direct routes are there?

Second idea. We can draw an arrow diagram. Copy and complete this arrow diagram (Figure 3) which shows the relation 'is linked by a direct route to'.

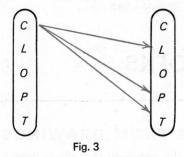

Fig. 3

Does the arrow diagram tell you how many routes (i) lead to Okehampton; (ii) start from Okehampton? How?

Third idea. We can make a table.

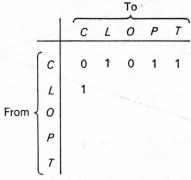

Fig. 4

This table, when completed, shows the number of routes linking each pair of towns.

Find *C* (down the side). Run your finger across until it is under *P* (along the top).

The entry in the table is 1. This shows that there is one route from C to P; check this from the map in Figure 1.

Check the other numbers in the table. Copy and complete the table.

A table which shows the number of routes between towns or the number of arcs between nodes is called a *route matrix*.

Look for patterns in your matrix and comment on those that you find.

(*c*) Which of the ideas in (*b*) shows the information most clearly? Which shows the information most concisely?

(*d*)

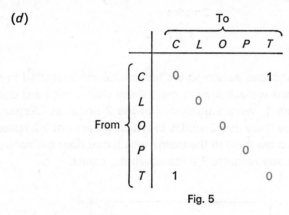

	To				
From	C	L	O	P	T
C	0			1	
L		0			
O			0		
P				0	
T	1				0

Fig. 5

Look at Figure 5. What can you say about the red numbers in the table? Why?

What can you say about the two black numbers? Why?

How are the black numbers related to the diagonal of 0's?

These 0's lie on the *leading diagonal* of the matrix.

(*e*) Copy and complete the matrix for Figure 6 (*a*). Why are there two routes from B to B?

Is the matrix symmetrical about the leading diagonal? Give a reason for your answer.

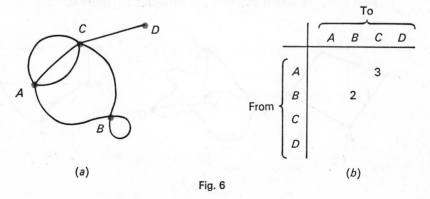

	To			
From	A	B	C	D
A			3	
B		2		
C				
D				

(*a*)   (*b*)

Fig. 6

99

(*f*) In *Book B* we found that on any given line segment we could mark as many 2-nodes as we please (see Figure 7).

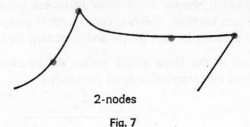

2-nodes

Fig. 7

In route diagrams and networks we are sometimes interested in some of the 2-nodes and we will always mark these with a large red dot. For example, in Figure 1, we are interested in the 2-nodes at Okehampton and Plymouth. Are there any 2-nodes in which we are not interested?

How many rows are there in the matrix which describes the network in Figure 8? How many columns? Write down the matrix.

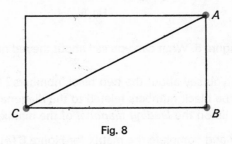

Fig. 8

Exercise A

1 Find matrices which describe the networks in Figure 9.

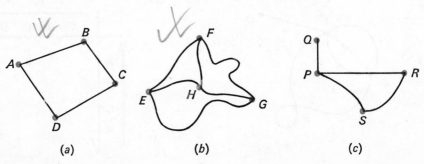

(*a*)   (*b*)   (*c*)

Fig. 9

2   Find matrices which describe the networks in Figure 10.

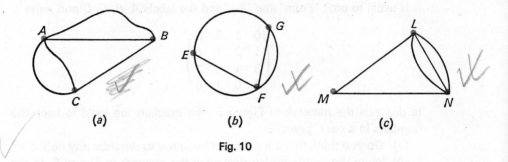

(a)   (b)   (c)

Fig. 10

3   Find the matrix which describes the topological map in Figure 11.

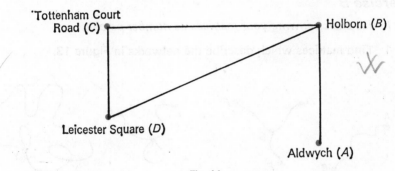

Fig. 11

4   Find matrices which describe the networks in Figure 12.

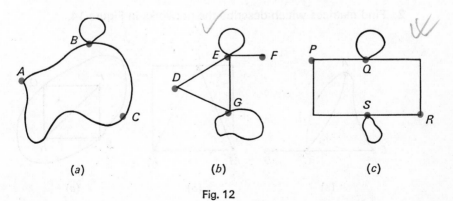

(a)   (b)   (c)

Fig. 12

101

1.1 Number parcels

It is usual to omit 'From' and 'To' and the labels *A, B, C, D* and write

$$\begin{pmatrix} 0 & 1 & 3 & 0 \\ 1 & 2 & 1 & 0 \\ 3 & 1 & 0 & 1 \\ 0 & 0 & 1 & 0 \end{pmatrix} \quad \checkmark$$

to describe the network in Figure 6. The brackets are used to keep the numbers in a neat 'parcel'.

(*a*) Do you think that a matrix can be found to describe any network?

(*b*) Write the matrix which describes the network in Figure 8, in the form of a number parcel.

Exercise B

In this exercise, write your matrices as number parcels.

1 Find matrices which describe the networks in Figure 13.

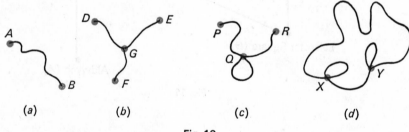

(*a*)   (*b*)   (*c*)   (*d*)

Fig. 13

2 Find matrices which describe the networks in Figure 14.

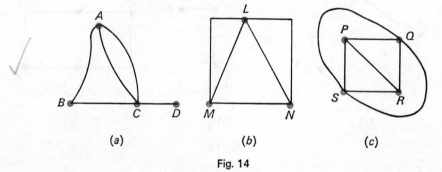

(*a*)   (*b*)   (*c*)

Fig. 14

3 (*a*) Figure 15 shows the network of roads on a small island. Write down the matrix which describes this network.

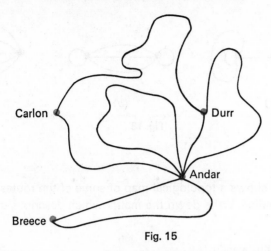

Fig. 15

(*b*) Draw some road networks of your own and write down the matrices which describe them. Ask your neighbour to check your results.

4 Figure 16 shows four networks with just two 3-nodes. Find the matrices which describe them. What do you notice?

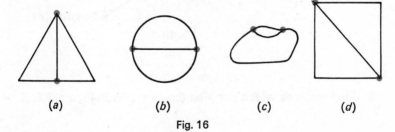

(*a*) (*b*) (*c*) (*d*)

Fig. 16

5 Figure 17 shows three networks with just four 3-nodes. Find the matrices which describe them. What do you notice?

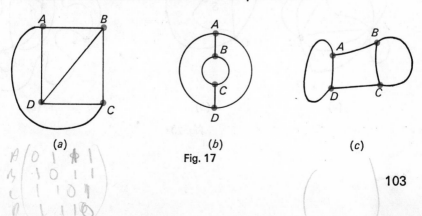

(*a*) (*b*) (*c*)

Fig. 17

103

6 The networks in Figure 18 have just two 5-nodes. Find the matrices which describe them. Comment on your results.

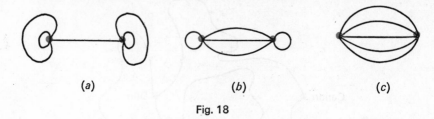

(a)   (b)   (c)

Fig. 18

7 Figure 19 shows a topological map of some of the routes of an international airline. Write down the matrix which describes the network.

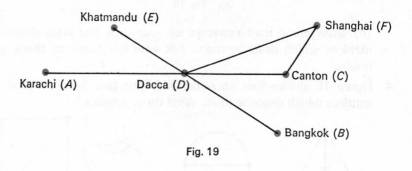

Fig. 19

8 Find matrices which describe the networks in Figure 20.

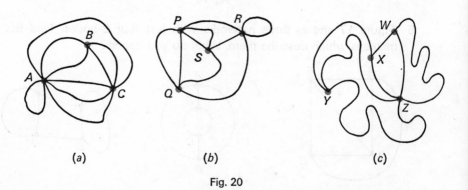

(a)   (b)   (c)

Fig. 20

9   Write down matrices which describe the maps in Figures 21 and 22.

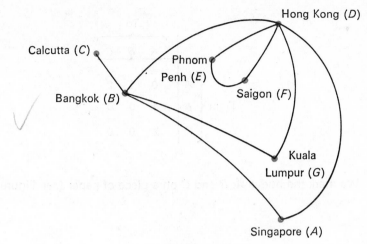

Fig. 21

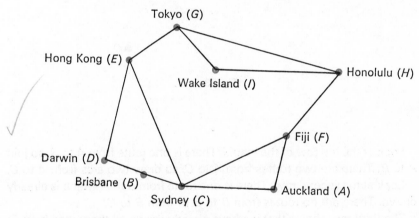

Fig. 22

2.   DRAWINGS FROM MATRICES

When we are given a network, we can find a matrix to describe it. We now think about the problem the other way round. Suppose we are given the route matrix

$$\begin{pmatrix} 0 & 1 & 2 \\ 1 & 0 & 0 \\ 2 & 0 & 0 \end{pmatrix}.$$

Can we draw the network it describes?

There are just three nodes. We will call them *A, B, C* and write the matrix in full:

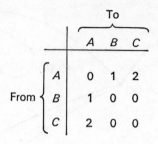

We mark the nodes *A, B* and *C* on a piece of paper (see Figure 23).

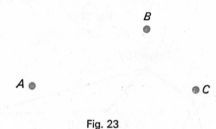

Fig. 23

Look at the top row of the matrix. There is one route from *A* to *B*, so join *A* to *B*. There are two routes from *A* to *C*, so draw two arcs from *A* to *C*.

Look at the second row. There is one route from *B* to *A* which is already drawn. There are no routes from *B* to *B* or from *B* to *C*.

The third row shows that we have already drawn all the routes from *C*. Figure 24 shows the completed network.

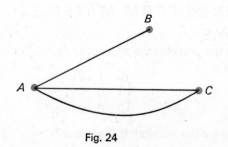

Fig. 24

(a) (i) There are three paths from *A*, so *A* is a 3-node. Describe the nodes at *B* and *C*.

(ii) Add up the numbers in each row of the matrix. What do you notice? Why does this happen?

(iii) Now add up the numbers in each column of the matrix. What do you find?

(b) (i) Call the nodes *A, B, C, D* and write in full the matrix

$$\begin{pmatrix} 0 & 1 & 1 & 1 \\ 1 & 0 & 0 & 1 \\ 1 & 0 & 0 & 0 \\ 1 & 1 & 0 & 0 \end{pmatrix}.$$

(ii) The top row of the matrix tells you that there are routes from *A* to *B*, *A* to *C* and *A* to *D* (see Figure 25). Copy and complete the network.

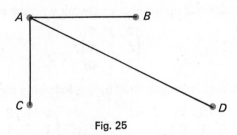

Fig. 25

(iii) Look at Figure 26. Which do you think is the best method of completing the network?

Are any of the drawings misleading? Why?

In Figure 26 (*d*) the route from *B* to *D* is shown as a flyover.

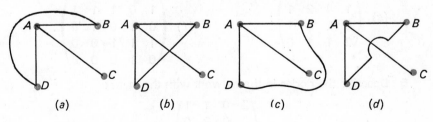

(*a*)   (*b*)   (*c*)   (*d*)

Fig. 26

Exercise C

1 Draw the networks described by the following matrices.

(a) $\begin{pmatrix} 0 & 0 & 1 \\ 0 & 0 & 1 \\ 1 & 1 & 0 \end{pmatrix}$; (b) $\begin{pmatrix} 0 & 1 & 2 \\ 1 & 0 & 1 \\ 2 & 1 & 0 \end{pmatrix}$; (c) $\begin{pmatrix} 0 & 2 & 2 \\ 2 & 0 & 2 \\ 2 & 2 & 0 \end{pmatrix}$.

Compare your networks with those drawn by your neighbour.

2 Draw the networks described by the following matrices.

(a) $\begin{pmatrix} 2 & 0 & 1 \\ 0 & 2 & 1 \\ 1 & 1 & 2 \end{pmatrix}$; (b) $\begin{pmatrix} 0 & 1 & 1 \\ 1 & 2 & 1 \\ 1 & 1 & 2 \end{pmatrix}$; (c) $\begin{pmatrix} 2 & 1 & 0 \\ 1 & 4 & 1 \\ 0 & 1 & 2 \end{pmatrix}$.

How do these networks differ from those in Question 1?

3 (a) Describe the nodes *A, B, C* for each of the networks in Question 1. Could you do this without first drawing the networks?
(b) Describe the nodes in the network with the matrix

$$\begin{pmatrix} 0 & 2 & 2 \\ 2 & 2 & 1 \\ 2 & 1 & 0 \end{pmatrix}.$$

4 Draw the networks described by the following matrices.

(a) $\begin{pmatrix} 0 & 1 & 0 & 1 \\ 1 & 0 & 1 & 0 \\ 0 & 1 & 0 & 1 \\ 1 & 0 & 1 & 0 \end{pmatrix}$; (b) $\begin{pmatrix} 0 & 1 & 2 & 1 \\ 1 & 0 & 1 & 0 \\ 2 & 1 & 0 & 1 \\ 1 & 0 & 1 & 0 \end{pmatrix}$;

(c) $\begin{pmatrix} 0 & 1 & 1 & 1 \\ 1 & 0 & 1 & 2 \\ 1 & 1 & 0 & 1 \\ 1 & 2 & 1 & 0 \end{pmatrix}$; (d) $\begin{pmatrix} 2 & 0 & 0 & 1 \\ 0 & 2 & 0 & 1 \\ 0 & 0 & 2 & 1 \\ 1 & 1 & 1 & 2 \end{pmatrix}$;

(e) $\begin{pmatrix} 0 & 1 & 0 & 2 \\ 1 & 4 & 2 & 1 \\ 0 & 2 & 0 & 1 \\ 2 & 1 & 1 & 0 \end{pmatrix}$; (f) $\begin{pmatrix} 0 & 1 & 0 & 1 & 0 \\ 1 & 0 & 1 & 1 & 1 \\ 0 & 1 & 0 & 1 & 0 \\ 1 & 1 & 1 & 0 & 0 \\ 0 & 1 & 0 & 0 & 0 \end{pmatrix}$.

5 Describe the nodes in the network with the matrix

$$\begin{pmatrix} 2 & 0 & 1 & 1 \\ 0 & 0 & 3 & 0 \\ 1 & 3 & 0 & 1 \\ 1 & 0 & 1 & 2 \end{pmatrix}.$$

Did you need to draw the network?

6 A network has four nodes *A, B, C, D* and *A* is a 3-node. What is the size of the matrix which describes this network? What can you say about the numbers in the first row of the matrix? What can you say about the numbers in the first column?

7 Draw a network and write down its matrix. Give the matrix to your neighbours and compare the networks which they draw from it with your own.

8 The numbers on the leading diagonal of a network matrix must be even or zero. Why?
A network has just two 3-nodes. Write down all the possible matrices which describe such a network. Draw the corresponding networks.

9 Write down all the possible matrices for a network with just two 5-nodes. Draw the networks.

10 Write down as many matrices as you can for a network with just two 7-nodes. Draw the networks.

11 Every one of four points is joined to every other. Write down the matrix which expresses this fact, and draw the network.

12 Repeat Question 11 with five points. What do you find when you draw the network? What do you think happens with six points?

3. DIRECTED MAPS

We can use the method of the previous section to find the matrix of a one-way street system. A map of a one-way system is called a *directed* map, because we have to put arrows on the roads to show in which direction we can go.

Figure 27 shows a directed map and the matrix which describes it.

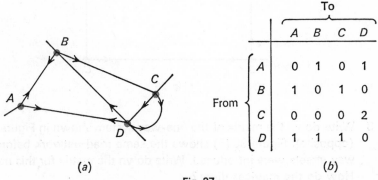

(a)   (b)

Fig. 27

(*a*) Check the numbers in the matrix.

(*b*) Describe the way in which the matrix of a directed map differs from the matrix of an undirected map.

Exercise D

1 Write down the matrices for the one-way street systems shown in Figure 28.

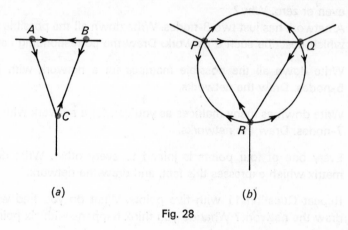

(*a*)   (*b*)

Fig. 28

2 Write down the matrix of the one-way street system shown in Figure 29. Ring the numbers that would be changed if the permitted directions along *AB* and *CD* were reversed.

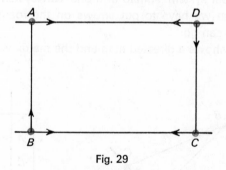

Fig. 29

3 Write down the matrix of the one-way system shown in Figure 30 (*a*) (opposite). Figure 30 (*b*) shows the same road network before one-way streets were introduced. Write down the matrix for this network. How do the matrices differ?

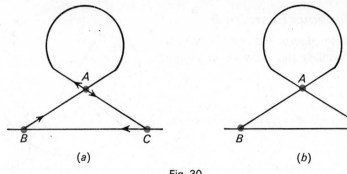

Fig. 30

4 Draw the one-way street system described by the matrix

$$\begin{pmatrix} 0 & 1 & 1 & 1 \\ 1 & 0 & 0 & 1 \\ 1 & 1 & 0 & 0 \\ 0 & 0 & 0 & 0 \end{pmatrix}.$$

What do the numbers on the bottom row tell you?

5 Draw a directed map of your own. Write down the matrix which describes it. Pass the matrix to your neighbours and ask them to draw the network. Compare their networks with yours.

6 (*a*) Write down the matrix of the one-way street system shown in Figure 31.

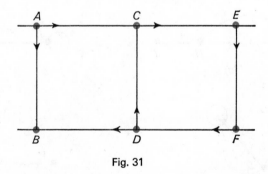

Fig. 31

(*b*) Why does the matrix contain a row of noughts?

(*c*) Why does the matrix contain a column of noughts?

(*d*) Ring the numbers that would be changed if the permitted directions along *AB*, *CD*, *EF* were reversed.

Miscellaneous Exercise E

1 Write down the matrix which describes the network in Figure 32.

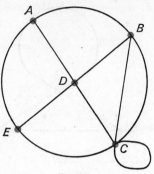

Fig. 32

2 Draw the networks described by the following matrices.

(a) $\begin{pmatrix} 2 & 1 & 1 \\ 1 & 2 & 3 \\ 1 & 3 & 4 \end{pmatrix}$;

(b) $\begin{pmatrix} 2 & 0 & 1 & 0 \\ 0 & 2 & 1 & 2 \\ 1 & 1 & 0 & 0 \\ 0 & 2 & 0 & 0 \end{pmatrix}$;

(c) $\begin{pmatrix} 0 & 3 & 1 & 0 & 1 \\ 3 & 0 & 2 & 0 & 1 \\ 1 & 2 & 0 & 1 & 0 \\ 0 & 0 & 1 & 4 & 1 \\ 1 & 1 & 0 & 1 & 0 \end{pmatrix}$.

3 Find matrices which describe the networks in Figure 33.

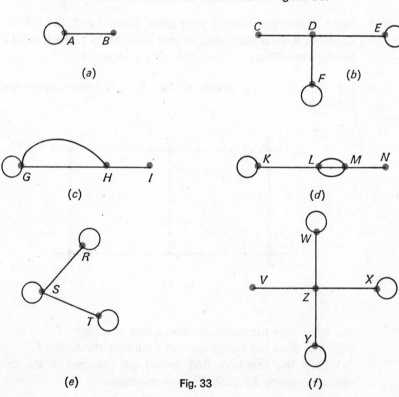

(a)

(b)

(c)

(d)

(e)

Fig. 33

(f)

4   Figure 34 shows a topological map of some of the routes of an airline. Write down the matrix which describes the network.

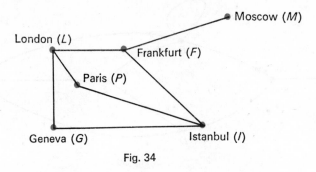

Fig. 34

5   Find matrices which describe the networks in Figure 35.

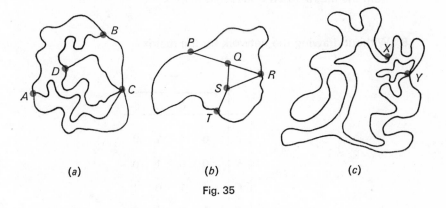

(a)   (b)   (c)

Fig. 35

6   Without drawing the network for the matrix

		To		
		A	*B*	*C*
From	*A*	2	1	2
	B	1	4	1
	C	2	1	0

(a) say whether there are any one-way routes;
(b) describe each of the nodes in the network.

7 (a) Write down the matrix for the one-way street system shown in Figure 36.

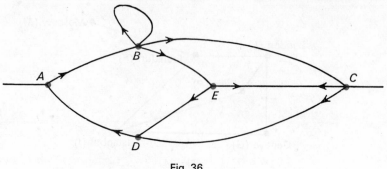

Fig. 36

(b) Describe the ways in which the matrix of a directed map differs from the matrix of an undirected map.

8 Without drawing the network for the matrix

		To			
		A	B	C	D
From	A	0	1	1	0
	B	0	0	1	0
	C	1	1	0	1
	D	1	0	1	0

state:

(a) whether there are any one-way routes;
(b) whether the path C–D–A is possible;
(c) whether the path C–B–A is possible.

*9 Draw the network described by the matrix

$$\begin{pmatrix} 2 & 0 & 1 & 0 \\ 0 & 0 & 0 & 2 \\ 1 & 0 & 0 & 0 \\ 0 & 2 & 0 & 2 \end{pmatrix}.$$

What happens?

*10 Euler's network formula states that $N + R = A + 2$, where N = number of nodes, R = number of regions and A = number of arcs. Consider the networks described by the matrices

(a) $\begin{pmatrix} 0 & 3 & 0 & 0 \\ 3 & 0 & 0 & 0 \\ 0 & 0 & 2 & 1 \\ 0 & 0 & 1 & 2 \end{pmatrix}$; (b) $\begin{pmatrix} 0 & 2 & 0 & 0 \\ 2 & 0 & 0 & 0 \\ 0 & 0 & 0 & 2 \\ 0 & 0 & 2 & 0 \end{pmatrix}$; (c) $\begin{pmatrix} 2 & 0 & 2 & 0 \\ 0 & 2 & 0 & 2 \\ 2 & 0 & 2 & 0 \\ 0 & 2 & 0 & 2 \end{pmatrix}$

and investigate whether Euler's formula is true for these networks. Draw other similar networks of your own and comment on your results.

*11 Write down all the possible matrices for a network with just four 3-nodes. Draw the corresponding networks. Some of them will have more than one branch, that is, they will be disconnected.

*12 (a) Draw, if possible, networks which have only the following:

    (i) one 1-node;
    (ii) one 3-node, one 4-node and one 5-node;
    (iii) two 3-nodes and one 1-node;
    (iv) five 1-nodes and one 5-node;
    (v) five 1-nodes and one 4-node.

(b) Describe, in terms of its nodes, a network which cannot be drawn. What happens when you try to write down the matrix?

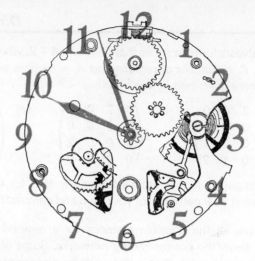

8. Rotations

1. INVESTIGATIONS

Investigation 1

You will need two coins of the same size. One coin A is held fixed. Another coin B rotates around it without slipping, starting in the position shown in Figure 1 (a), with its head upright. When it gets to the position of Figure 1 (b) will its head be upright or upside down? Try it and see.

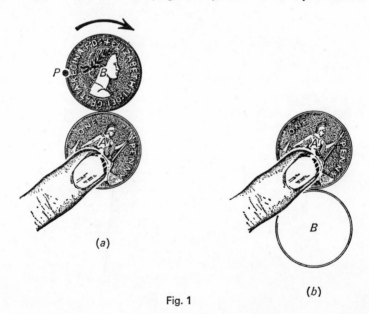

(a)

(b)

Fig. 1

What is the path traced out by a point *P* on coin *B* as it rotates about coin *A*?

Investigate this also with two other coins of the same size.

Investigation 2

You may have seen a Spirograph. It is a fascinating device in which one circle rotates around another. Here are some patterns which can be obtained. Find out more about it.

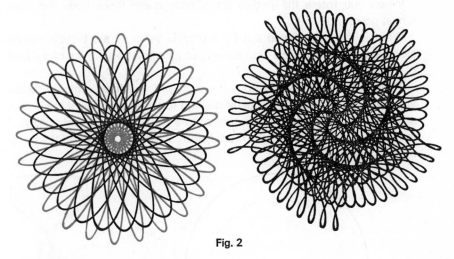

Fig. 2

Investigation 3

Cut out any shape from a piece of card (see Figure 3). Put a pin through it at some point *O* and make a small hole for a pencil to go through at another point *P*. Rotate the cut-out and mark the path of *P* with the pencil.

What is the path of *P*?

If *Q* is any other point on the cut-out, what can you say about the path of *Q*?

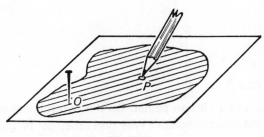

Fig. 3

Investigation 4

There is a theory that when water goes down a plughole in the northern hemisphere it rotates clockwise. Investigate this.

Investigation 5

Take a look at a bicycle.
Make a list of all the rotating parts.
When you rotate the pedals once, how many times does the back wheel go round?
What is the path traced out by a bicycle valve as the bicycle travels along a road? What is the path traced out by a point on the rim of a wheel of a railway engine?
To investigate these questions it will help if you have a model. Make yourself a flanged wheel, either by sticking together 2 circles of thick card, or by sticking a circle of thick card onto a tin lid. Make 3 holes X, Y, Z to take a pencil point. Roll the model along a ledge, and so find the paths of X, Y and Z.

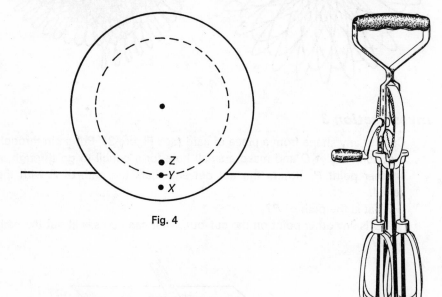

Fig. 4

Fig. 5

Investigation 6

Take a look at a kitchen beater. Do the two rotating parts of the beater rotate in the same direction? Why don't they get tangled up? If you turn the handle once, how many times do the beaters turn?

2. PROPERTIES OF ROTATIONS

You will need : tracing paper,
a pin or compass point.

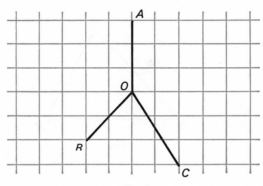

Fig. 6

(*a*) Copy Figure 6 into your book. Put a piece of tracing paper on top of your diagram, and trace it through. Leave the tracing paper in position and, with a pin or compass point, rotate the tracing paper about *O* so that *OA* goes through an angle of 90°.

   (i)   Through what angle has *OB* rotated?

   (ii) Through what angle has *OC* rotated?

   (iii) If *OA* had been rotated through 60°, what angle would *OB* and *OC* have gone through?

(*b*) Copy Figure 7 into your book. Using tracing paper as in (*a*), rotate it about *O* so that *OE* moves through 90°.

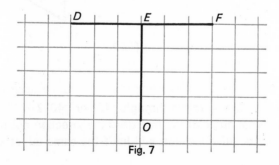

Fig. 7

   (i)   What is the angle between the old and the new directions of *DEF*?

   (ii) If *OE* was rotated through 30°, what would be the angle between the old and the new directions of *DEF*?

(*c*) Copy Figure 8 into your book and using tracing paper as before, rotate it about *O* so that *OG* goes through an angle of 40°. What is the angle between the old and new directions of *GH*?

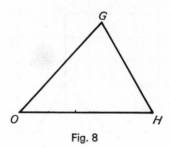

Fig. 8

(*d*) When you rotated your tracing paper did you rotate clockwise or anticlockwise?

In order that everyone agrees, it is necessary to state the direction of rotation. This is often done by saying that an anticlockwise rotation is positive, and a clockwise rotation is negative.

Fig. 9

(i)   In (*c*) did you rotate through +40° or −40°?

(ii) For what angle of rotation does the direction not matter?

(iii) What positive rotation will have the same effect as a rotation of −100°?

(*e*) Copy Figure 8 again. This time we are going to rotate it through +40° about a point, *C*. To do this join *CG*. Use your protractor, and mark an angle of +40° as in Figure 10 (opposite).

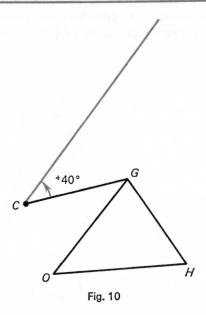

Fig. 10

Now put your tracing paper on top and rotate it about *C* until *G* lies on the red line. Dot through the new positions of *G*, *H* and *O*.

Exercise A

1   Copy Figure 11 into your book, and rotate:

(*a*) *AB* through $+90°$ about O_1;

(*b*) *CD* through $+90°$ about O_2;

(*c*) *EF* through $-90°$ about O_3.

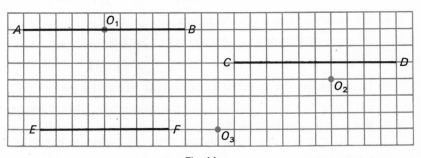

Fig. 11

2 Copy Figure 12 into your book. Rotate *ABC* about *O* through ⁺50°.
(*Hint:* join *OA* ; mark *OA'* so that *AOA'* = ⁺50°.)

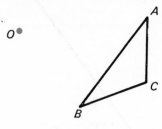

Fig. 12

What is the angle between the old and the new directions of
(*a*) *AB* ; (*b*) *BC* ; (*c*) *CA*?

Fig. 13

3 Copy Mr Poly (Figure 13) and rotate him through ⁻40° about *O*.

4 Draw a shape of your own. State an angle and a centre of rotation and get your neighbour to rotate the shape.

5 Give another angle of rotation which would have the same effect as a rotation of

(*a*) ⁺35° ;   (*b*) ⁺123° ;   (*c*) ⁻42° ;
(*d*) ⁺315° ;   (*e*) ⁺227° ;   (*f*) ⁻148°.

6 On squared paper mark the points

$$A\ (^+2,\ ^+1),\quad B\ (^+3,\ ^+4),\quad C\ (^-2,\ ^+3),$$
$$D\ (^-3,\ ^-1),\quad E\ (^+2,\ ^-2),\quad F\ (0,\ ^+1).$$

Using tracing paper, rotate through 180° about the origin (0, 0).

(*a*) What are the coordinates of the new points? What happens to the coordinates each time?

(*b*) If a point has coordinates (^+a, ^+b), what will be its new coordinates?

7   Repeat Question 6 but rotate through an angle of ⁺90°.

8   Copy Figure 14.

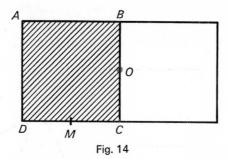

Fig. 14

If the shaded square is rotated through 180° about *O*, it will map onto the unshaded square.

(*a*) Draw in the paths which *C*, *D* and *M* will follow during this rotation.

(*b*) What other centres of rotation could be used to map one square onto the other? Give the angle of rotation for each centre.

(*c*) In what other ways could you map one square onto the other?

9   In each diagram of Figure 15, the shaded flag has to be rotated onto the unshaded flag.
Copy the flags, and put in the centres of rotation.
Give the positive angle of rotation in each case.

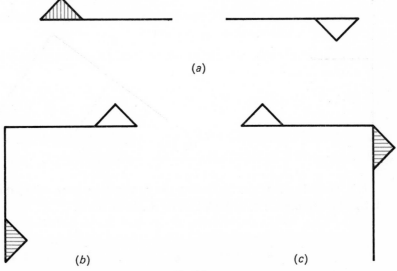

(*a*)

(*b*)   (*c*)

Fig. 15

3. CENTRES OF ROTATION

(*a*) Using tracing paper, copy Figure 16 (*a*) into your book. By trial and error with a pin or compass point, see if you can find a point so that when you rotate your tracing paper, one *F* maps onto the other. What do you notice about the position of this centre of rotation?

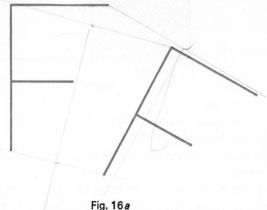

Fig. 16*a*

(*b*) Repeat for Figure 16 (*b*). This time you will find that the centre of rotation is not at the intersection of the 'uprights' of the *F*'s.

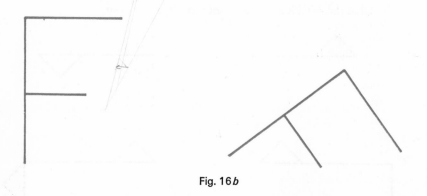

Fig. 16*b*

(*c*) There is a method for finding the centre of rotation without doing it by trial and error. Let us look at how it can be done.

A   O   B

Fig. 17

If *A* rotates onto *B*, then *O* is a possible centre of rotation. Try to find some more.

(*Hint:* copy Figure 17 onto tracing paper and fold so that *A* maps onto *B*.)

Suppose *P* is a point on the fold. What can you say about *PA* and *PB*? Where are all the possible centres of rotation?

Here is Figure 16 (*b*) again with some points labelled. Copy it onto tracing paper.

P has to rotate onto *P'*: find the position of all the possible centres of rotation by folding your paper.

In the same way, *Q* has to rotate onto *Q'*. Again fold your paper. Where must the centre of rotation, *O*, be so that *PQ* maps onto *P'Q'*?

With this centre of rotation, try to explain in your own words why *R* must rotate onto *R'*.

Fold your paper so that *R* maps onto *R'*, and check that the fold passes through *O*.

Exercise B

1 By folding tracing paper find the centre of rotation so that the shaded flag maps onto the unshaded one (Figure 18).

Fig. 18

2 Trace the boots in Figure 19. By folding, find the centre of rotation so that *A* maps onto *A′*, and *B* onto *B′*.

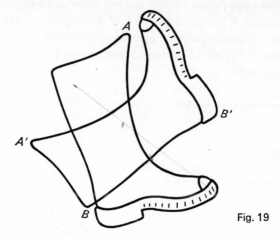

Fig. 19

3 The map in Figure 20 has been rotated about a certain point. By tracing it and folding the tracing paper, find the centre of rotation.

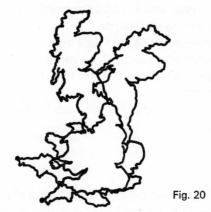

Fig. 20

4 In Figures 21 (*a*) and (*b*), is it possible to map one *F* onto the other by a rotation?

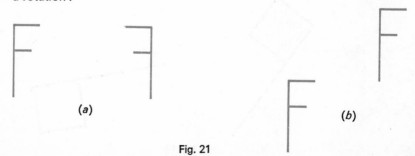

(*a*)

(*b*)

Fig. 21

5 Draw a shape of your own design in two positions and ask your neighbour to find the centre of rotation.

6 *How a draughtsman would find a centre of rotation using compasses.* Suppose he wants to find where all the possible centres of rotation are so that *A* maps onto *A'*. He would draw 2 equal circles with centres at *A* and *A'*.

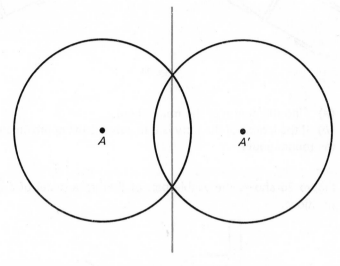

Fig. 22

Then the red line gives the position of all the possible centres of rotation. Try to explain why this works.

Copy Figure 23, and repeat this construction for *P* and *P'*, *Q* and *Q'*, and also for *R* and *R'*. Do your three lines meet at a point?

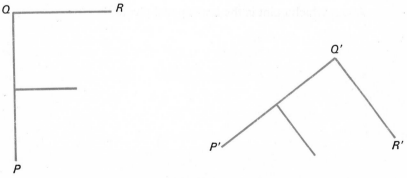

Fig. 23

7 Figure 24 gives a bird's eye view of the position at two different moments of a lorry being driven round a roundabout.

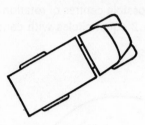 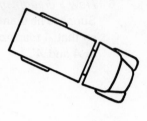

Fig. 24

(*a*) Find the centre of the roundabout.

(*b*) If the length of the lorry is 6 m, what is the approximate radius of the roundabout?

8 Figure 25 shows the visible part of the brake pedal of a car in two positions.

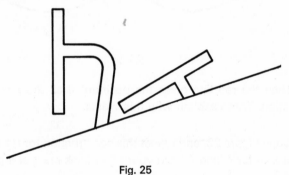

Fig. 25

About which point is the brake pedal pivoted?

Miscellaneous Exercise C

1   Figure 26 is a picture of the big wheel at a fair. Jean gets in at the bottom when Anne is half-way up.

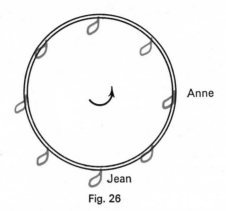

Anne

Jean

Fig. 26

(*a*) When Anne is at the top where will Jean be? What angle will the wheel have rotated through then?

(*b*) What angle will the wheel have rotated through when Jean is directly above Anne?

2   A see-saw consists of a plank *AB*, pivoted at a point *C*, as shown in Figure 27. Trace it into your book. Then, by putting a pin or compass point through *C*, rotate the tracing paper until *B* is touching the ground. Through what angle has the plank rotated?

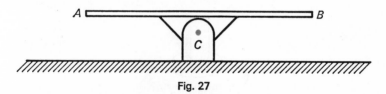

Fig. 27

3   Figure 28 shows a simple adding machine. To add 3 and 4 you first slide the 3 stick along and then the 4 stick. 7 clocks up. Through what angle will the wheel have rotated?

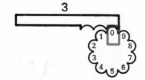

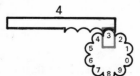

Fig. 28

129

You could make a model of this. Can you work out a method for carrying to a 'tens' wheel?

4   Look at Figure 29.

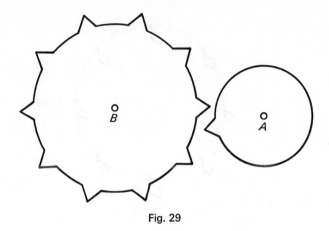

Fig. 29

(*a*) If wheel *A* rotates clockwise, in which direction will wheel *B* rotate?

(*b*) When wheel *A* makes one complete turn, how much of a turn will wheel *B* have made?

(*c*) Try to work out how this principle could be used in a calculating machine.

5   (*a*)   In Figure 30, if *A* has 40 cogs and *B* has 30 cogs, how many times does *B* rotate when *A* makes three complete turns?

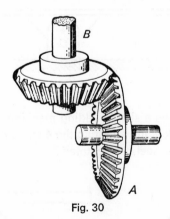

Fig. 30

(*b*) *C* has 50 cogs. Each turn of *D* rotates *C* through 20 cogs. How many turns of *D* make *C* go through a complete turn?

6 An 'up-and-over' garage door *AB* (seen edge on in Figure 31) moves about a horizontal axis through *C*.

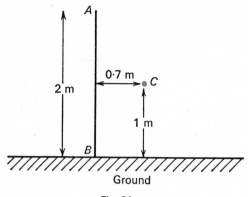

Fig. 31

With the dimensions shown, draw a diagram showing the position of the door when raised.

What height is the tallest vehicle which could use the garage?

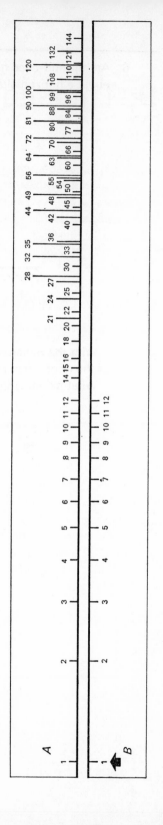

9. The slide rule

Some time ago you might have had difficulty in remembering your multiplication tables, and you might even have copied out a multiplication square to help you learn them.

Here is a device which can be used to give all the multiplication tables up to 12 times 12.

Copy, very carefully, the two scales opposite onto two strips of stiff paper or card.

1. HOW IT WORKS

In Figure 1, the scales have been set to show the two-times table.

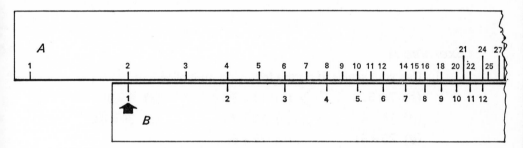

Fig. 1

Make sure that you can use the scales to do all the multiplication tables up to 12 times 12.

The flow diagram in Figure 2 shows the route you take when doing the multiplication 2×3 with these scales:

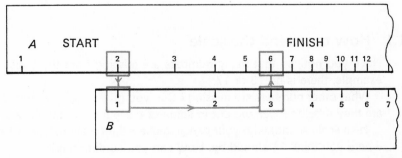

Fig. 2

133

Suppose you set the scales for multiplication as above, but went the other way round (see Figure 3).

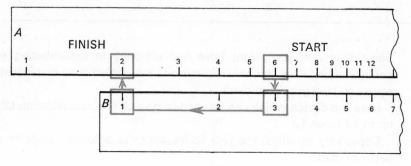

Fig. 3

What operation are the scales now performing?

Exercise A

1 Use your scales to do the following multiplications:

(a) 7×5;   (b) 11×8;   (c) 9×9;

(d) 14×4;   (e) 18×3;   (f) 30×4;

(g) 25×3;   (h) 27×5.

2 Use your scales to do the following divisions:

(a) $14 \div 7$;   (b) $60 \div 10$;   (c) $21 \div 3$;

(d) $64 \div 8$;   (e) $56 \div 7$;   (f) $108 \div 12$;

(g) $24 \div 6$;   (h) $121 \div 11$.

1.1 How to extend the scale

Have you noticed that many numbers are missing from the scales? For example, there is no 13 or 17.

What other numbers are missing? Can you give a name to them? Why are they missing? Can we put in some of these missing numbers?

Take scale A and, with your pencil, make a light mark between 1 and 2 where you think $1\frac{1}{2}$ should be. How can you confirm this?

Set your scales to show $3 \div 2$. (See Figure 4 opposite.)

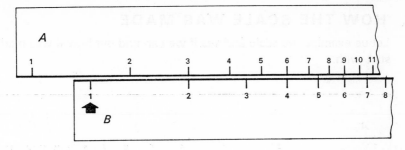

Fig. 4

Notice that $1\frac{1}{2}$ is *not* half way between 1 and 2.

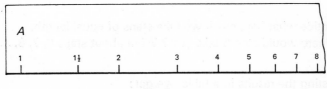

Fig. 5

Notice also that the gap between 1 and 2 is not the same as the gap between 2 and 3, and that the gap between 2 and 3 is not the same as the gap between 3 and 4 and so on.

Exercise B

1 Write the following mixed numbers as fractions and use your answer to mark each point on scale *A*.

(a) $2\frac{1}{2}$;   (b) $3\frac{1}{2}$;   (c) $4\frac{1}{2}$;   (d) $5\frac{1}{2}$;

(e) $1\frac{1}{4}$;   (f) $2\frac{1}{4}$;   (g) $6\frac{1}{4}$;   (h) $1\frac{3}{4}$.

2 Use an accurate method to mark the following extra points on scale *A*.

(a) 75;   (b) 105;   (c) 140;   (d) 126.

3 Can you find a way to place 13 accurately on the scale?

2. HOW THE SCALE WAS MADE

Let us examine the scale and see if we can find out how it was made to start with.

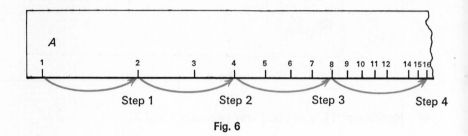

Fig. 6

Notice what happens if we take steps of equal length.
Where would step 5 take you? What about steps 6, 7, 8, ..., n?

Listing the results in a table, we get:

Step number	1	2	3	4	5	6	7	. . .	n
Scale number	2	4	8	16	32	64	128	. . .	?

What scale number corresponds to step number n? To answer this we must notice that the scale numbers can be written as powers of 2. The table then becomes:

Step number	1	2	3	4	5	6	7	. . .	n
Scale number	2^1	2^2	2^3	2^4	2^5	2^6	2^7	. . .	2^n

and we see that step n corresponds to scale number 2^n.

We can investigate this relationship even further if a graph is drawn, showing:

$$\text{step number} \rightarrow \text{scale number,}$$

that is,
$$x \rightarrow 2^x.$$

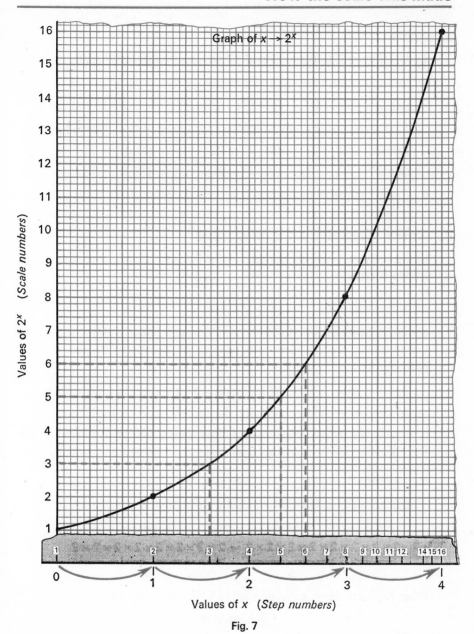

Fig. 7

Now you can see how the scale was constructed, and how points in between the step numbers were obtained. At last you can enter 13 and 17, in fact, all the numbers missing from your scale.

Notice that step 0 corresponds to a scale number of 1, and so we shall take the value of 2^0 as 1.

137

Exercise C

1   Use Figure 7 to mark 13 and 17 on your scale.

2   Use the graph to try and find meanings for:

(a) $2^{\frac{1}{2}}$;   (b) $2^{1\frac{1}{2}}$;   (c) $2^{\frac{3}{4}}$;   (d) $2^{2 \cdot 5}$;   (e) $2^{3\frac{1}{2}}$;   (f) $2^{0 \cdot 8}$.

3   Find the value of x which makes each of the following relations true:

(a) $2^x = 8$;   (b) $2^x = 2$;   (c) $2^x = 3$;

(d) $2^x = 6$;   (e) $2^x = 10$;   (f) $2^x = 2\frac{1}{2}$.

4   Could the graph be used to find a meaning for 2^{-1}?

3. WHY THE SCALE WORKS

In the early seventeenth century, John Napier was working with calculations such as

$$4 \times 32 = 128$$

or, in powers of 2, $2^2 \times 2^5 = 2^7,$

and he noticed something interesting. Can you see what it is? If not, put the following calculations into powers of 2 and try to see what is happening.

(a) $8 \times 16 = 128$;   (b) $4 \times 16 = 64$;   (c) $4 \times 64 = 256$;

(d) $2 \times 32 = 64$;   (e) $8 \times 32 = 256$.

You should notice that when a multiplication such as $8 \times 32 = 256$ is put into powers of 2:

$$2^3 \times 2^5 = 2^8,$$

the indices are *added:* $3 + 5 = 8.$

This can be checked by writing the calculation out in full:

$$
\begin{array}{ccccc}
2^3 & \times & 2^5 & = & 2^8 \\
\underbrace{2 \times 2 \times 2}_{3} \times & \underbrace{2 \times 2 \times 2 \times 2 \times 2}_{5} & = & \underbrace{2 \times 2 \times 2 \times 2 \times 2 \times 2 \times 2 \times 2}_{8}
\end{array}
$$

What happens when a division is put into powers of 2?

$$128 \div 16 = 8,$$

$$2^7 \div 2^4 = 2^3.$$

If we have the two sequences

0	1	2	3	4	5	6	7	8	9	...
$\updownarrow$	$\updownarrow$	$\updownarrow$	$\updownarrow$	$\updownarrow$	$\updownarrow$	$\updownarrow$	$\updownarrow$	$\updownarrow$	$\updownarrow$	
1	2	4	8	16	32	64	128	256	512	...

and we match corresponding pairs, then multiplication and division can be converted into the far easier operations of addition and subtraction. This is the foundation of Napier's discovery.

For example, to do the *multiplication* 8×32 we find the numbers corresponding to 8 and 32 in the first sequence and *add* them

$$8 \longrightarrow 3$$
$$\underline{32 \longrightarrow 5}$$
$$\text{add } 8$$

Now work backwards and find the number corresponding to 8 in the second sequence:

$$256 \longleftarrow 8.$$

Answer, $8 \times 32 = 256$.

Figure 8 shows the process once again, set out in a flow diagram.

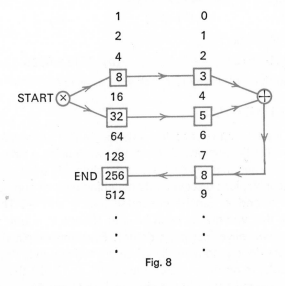

Fig. 8

Likewise, to do the *division* $256 \div 4$ we need to change to the other sequence and do the *subtraction* $8-2$. This gives the answer 6 which corresponds to 64. Final answer, $256 \div 4 = 64$.

Draw a flow diagram like the one above to show this.

Exercise D

1 Write out the two sequences as in Figure 8 and draw the flow diagram for the calculations:

   (*a*) $4 \times 16 = 64$;   (*b*) $512 \div 64 = 8$.

2 Calculate, leaving your answers in powers of 2:

(a) $2^2 \times 2^3$;　　(b) $2^7 \times 2^3$;　　(c) $2^1 \times 2^5$;　　(d) $2^0 \times 2^4$;

(e) $2^3 \times 2^3$;　　(f) $2^3 \times 2^2 \times 2^4$.

3 Calculate, leaving your answers in powers of 2:

(a) $2^7 \div 2^5$;　　　　(b) $2^5 \div 2^3$;　　　　　(c) $2^8 \div 2^2$;

(d) $2^4 \div 2^3$;　　　　(e) $2^3 \div 2^3$.

4 What is 2^{12}?

5 Calculate, by changing into powers of 2 and then changing back again for the answer:

(a) 4×8;　　　　(b) 4×64;　　　　(c) 8×32;

(d) 16×16;　　　(e) 8×128;　　　(f) $64 \div 8$;

(g) $256 \div 4$;　　　(h) $512 \div 128$;　　(i) $1024 \div 64$.

6 Given that $2^{25} = 33\,554\,432$ find:

(a) 2^{24};　　　　　　(b) 2^{23};　　　　　　　(c) 2^{26}.

7 Multiply together:

(a) 1024×512;　　　　　　(b) 2048×4096.

Can you think of a way to check your anwers?

4. THE SLIDE RULE

When you were using your scales at the beginning of the chapter to help you to do multiplication and division, you were using a simple slide rule.

We can now see that the scales on your slide rule were constructed by making use of Napier's discovery. By matching pairs of numbers from two sequences, $\times$ and $\div$ can be converted into $+$ and $-$. The scales are arranged so that you do not even have to change from one sequence to another (as you have just been doing). Even the simple operations of $+$ and $-$ are done automatically when your slide rule is set.

For example, to do the *multiplication* $3 \times 4 = 12$, set the scales in the way we discovered earlier in the chapter (see Figure 9).

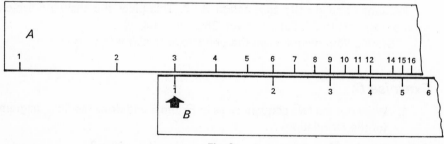

Fig. 9

We see that the length of rule corresponding to 3 is added to the length corresponding to 4. This gives the length corresponding to 12.

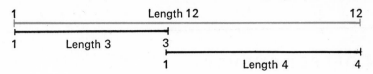

Fig. 10. Length 3 + length 4 = length 12.

Exercise E

1   Draw diagrams similar to the one in Figure 10 to show these calculations:

(*a*) $2 \times 5 = 10$;   (*b*) $4 \times 4 = 16$;   (*c*) $20 \div 5 = 4$;

(*d*) $18 \div 6 = 3$;   (*e*) $2 \times 3\frac{1}{2} = 7$.

2   Use your scales to do these calculations:

(*a*) $1\frac{1}{2} \times 3$;   (*b*) $1\frac{1}{4} \times 4$;   (*c*) $2\frac{1}{2} \times 2\frac{1}{2}$;

(*d*) $6 \div 4$;   (*e*) $9 \div 2$;   (*f*) $10 \div 8$.

3   Use the graph on page 137 to find a meaning for:

(*a*) $2^{2\frac{1}{4}}$;   (*b*) $2^{3\frac{1}{2}}$;   (*c*) $2^{0 \cdot 6}$;   (*d*) $2^{1 \cdot 7}$.

4   Find the value of *x* which makes each of the following relations true:

(*a*) $2^x = 4$;   (*b*) $2^x = 5$;   (*c*) $2^x = 9$;   (*d*) $2^x = 1\frac{1}{2}$.

5   Make a copy of the graph in Figure 7 and extend it so that you can read off values for:

(*a*) 2^{-1};   (*b*) 2^{-2};   (*c*) 2^{-3};   (*d*) $2^{-\frac{1}{2}}$.

6   Calculate, leaving your answers in powers of 2:

(*a*) $2^5 \times 2^3$;   (*b*) $2^4 \times 2^6$;   (*c*) $2^{1\frac{1}{2}} \times 2^{2\frac{1}{2}}$;

(*d*) $2^4 \times 2^{-1}$;   (*e*) $2^{-1} \times 2^{-3}$;   (*f*) $2^7 \div 2^3$.

7   Work out the values of:

(*a*) 2^{10};   (*b*) 2^{14}.

8   Calculate by changing into powers of 2 and then changing back again for the answer:

(*a*) 4×32;   (*b*) 16×64;   (*c*) 32×32;

(*d*) $128 \div 8$;   (*e*) $4096 \div 256$.

Interlude

AN OFFSET SURVEY

The diagram below shows a patch of lawn in a school garden. No doubt you can think of several such areas in your own school or home garden.

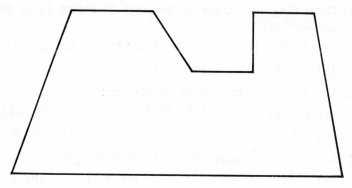

Fig. 1

The following instructions suggest how you would go about making a survey without using any special equipment.

(i)   Choose the area that you and your group are going to survey and make a sketch of its outline in your notebook.

(ii) Find the longest possible straight edge of this area and call this your survey line. (*AM* in Figure 2.)

(iii) Use a toe to heel method for measuring, calling one shoe-length a unit, and carry out *offset* measurements from the survey line to the corners of your area (such as *BP*, *CQ*, etc., in Figure 2). Record these distances in shoe-lengths in your notebook.

The offsets are judged by eye to be at right-angles to the survey line at a measured distance along it.

Diagram as in your notebook   *Offset lines are dotted*

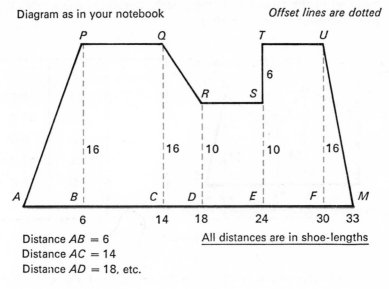

Distance $AB = 6$ All distances are in shoe-lengths
Distance $AC = 14$
Distance $AD = 18$, etc.

Fig. 2

Inside the classroom

Measure your shoe-length to the nearest centimetre. Copy and fill in the table below and use it to help you to convert shoe-lengths to centimetres.

Number of shoe-lengths	1	2	4	8	16	32	64
Lengths in centimetres							

When you have chosen a suitable scale, draw a diagram of the surveyed area in your exercise book, putting the distances in metres on your final diagram as in Figure 3.

143

Further experiments in surveying

Consider the survey shown in Figure 3 and then see if you can give any meaning to the table beside the sketch. Surveyors use a table like this when working on building sites.

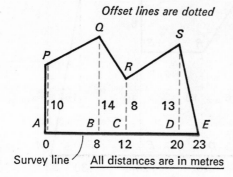

	E	
	23	0 *E*
	20	13 *S*
	12	8 *R*
	8	14 *Q*
	0	10 *P*
	A	

Fig. 3

Make a table similar in lay-out to the one above for your survey.

When judging right-angles by eye, why do you think that it is advisable to keep offsets as short as possible?

CODES

Perhaps the simplest way of producing a code is to replace each letter of the alphabet by a number and the easiest choice would be to let

$$A = 1, \quad B = 2, \quad C = 3, \quad D = 4, \quad E = 5, \text{ etc.}$$

A	B	C	D	E	F	G	H	I	J	K	L	M	N	O	P	Q	R	S	T	U	V	W	X	Y	Z
1	2	3	4	5	6	7	8	9	10	11	12	13	14	15	16	17	18	19	20	21	22	23	24	25	26

The message
FOOD URGENTLY NEEDED

would then be sent as

6, 15, 15, 4, 21, 18, 7, 5, 14, 20, 12, 25, 14, 5, 5, 4, 5, 4.

Once you had converted the numbers to letters it would be fairly easy to tell where one word ended and the next began.

If you wanted to make the code harder to crack, you could, for example, add three to each number. The message would then be sent as

9, 18, 18, 7, 24, 21, 10, 8, 17, 23, 15, (2), 17, 8, 8, 7, 8, 7.

(Notice the ringed 2. What number is it replacing? Why?)

If you wrote $x + 3$ at the end, this would tell the receiver how to decode the message.

Try to decipher the following messages for yourself.

10, 19, 10, 18, 4, 6, 12, 10, 19, 25, 8, 6, 21, 25, 26, 23, 10, 9, $x + 5$.

7, 12, 3, 3, 2, 25, 12, 13, 18, 6, 3, 16, 18, 6, 13, 19, 17, 25, 12, 2, 14, 13, 19, 12, 2, 17, $x - 2$.

2, 15, 19, 24, 16, 25, 2, 13, 15, 23, 15, 24, 4, 3, 11, 2, 2, 19, 6, 15, 4, 25, 23, 25, 2, 2, 25, 7, $x + 10$.

10, 6, 25, 21, 13, 25, 13, 25, 8, 24, 7, 9, 12, 25, 1, 15, 8, 13, $x - 6$.

2, 24, 24, 18, 2, 14, 4, 4, 8, 16, 10, 2, 24, 14, 16, $2x$.

Now write a message in a code of your own choice and see if a friend can decode it correctly.

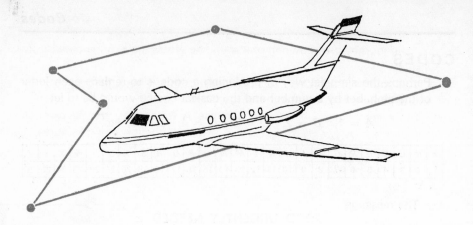

10. Journeys

You will need :
a protractor,
a ruler,
a *sharp* pencil.

A pilot makes a two-stage journey :

        Stage 1 : 500 km, bearing 060° ;

        Stage 2 : 300 km, bearing 150°.

Here is a scale drawing to show his route :

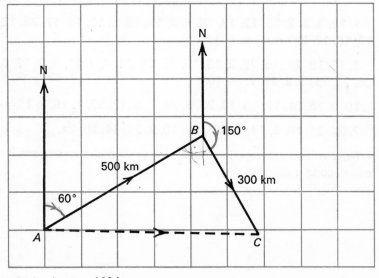

Scale : 1 cm = 100 km   Fig. 1

If the journey was flown in one stage, he would have gone direct from *A* to *C*.

Use your protractor and ruler to measure this. Check that it comes to approximately 580 km on a bearing of 091°.

There are some questions in Exercise A for you to try. Remember, bearings are always measured in a <u>clockwise</u> direction from the <u>north</u>.

Squared paper may help.

State your scale in each case.

Exercise A

1 A boat takes the following course:

600 km, bearing 150°,

followed by   800 km, bearing 050°.

If it were possible, what distance and bearing would the boat need to take if the journey was to be completed in one stage?

2 A pilot is asked to fly:

400 km, bearing 250°,

followed by   600 km, bearing 300°.

Find what single journey would have taken him from his starting point to his destination.

3 Figure 2 shows the path of a hockey ball (not drawn to scale). Find the distance *AC* and the angle *NAC*.

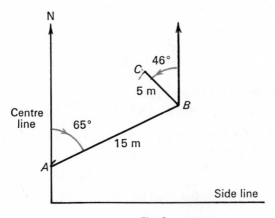

Fig. 2

4   A pilot wants to fly from *A* to *B*, a distance of 1200 km, and *B* is on a bearing of 082° from *A*. Due to bad weather, the pilot makes a detour and refuels at *C*. The distance between *A* and *C* is 700 km and the bearing of *C* from *A* is 175°. Find the distance from *C* to *B*, and the bearing which the pilot has to take.

5   (500, 090°) stands for a journey of 500 km on a bearing of 090°. Find the single journey represented by:

$$(500, 090°),$$

$$\text{followed by} \quad (375, 250°).$$

6   A rocket first rises 20 km vertically, then 80 km at 30° from the vertical and finally 60 km at 70° from the vertical. Find how high it is then above the launching pad.

7   A pilot is to make a 'round trip' calling at three airports, *B*, *C* and *D*, before returning to base *A*. Figure 3 shows a *sketch* of the route he takes.

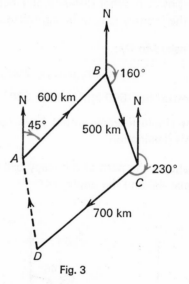

Fig. 3

Which airport is nearest to *A*?

What bearing must the pilot take to return straight from *D* to *A*?

8   (60, 050°) stands for a journey of 60 km on a bearing of 050°. Find the single journey represented by:

$$(60, 050°),$$

$$\text{followed by} \quad (40, 320°),$$

$$\text{followed by} \quad (45, 260°).$$

11. Statistics

1. CHOOSING A REPRESENTATIVE VALUE

In the first chapter on Statistics in *Book B* we saw how we could collect and display information. In this chapter we shall examine some of the ways of selecting a typical value to represent such information.

This is just like electing a form captain or a school council delegate, where one person is chosen to represent a large group of people.

Think of some of the ways in which you could choose a form representative:

   (i)   the most popular;
  (ii)   the tallest;
 (iii)   the strongest;
 (iv)   the fastest runner;
  (v)   the name picked from a hat,

and many others.

Sometimes we should have reason to choose one of these and sometimes another.

Suggest some situations when you need to choose a representative, and in each case explain how and why you make the choice. Was the representative usually typical of the group you were choosing from?

In statistics we also need to choose representatives, and again there are many ways of doing this.

Project

  (*a*) Measure the height (to the nearest centimetre) of each member of the class. Discuss carefully how you will make the measurements before you start. Choose one person to do the measuring and another to record the heights.

(*b*) We now want to choose one reading to represent all the others. Find a representative value using each of the methods suggested below.

(i)   Choose the greatest height.

(ii)   Choose the least height.

(iii)   Choose the height 'in between' these two.

(iv)   Choose the most common height.

(v)   Line up the class in order of height, and choose the height of the pupil who is in the middle of the line.

(vi)   Find the total height of all the pupils in the class and divide this by the number of pupils in the class.

Which of these heights would you choose as being the most *typical* of the members of your class?

Now let us use the same methods of choosing a representative value for the heights of a specially selected set of pupils.

Example 1

The heights in centimetres of 21 girls were measured, and the results were

167	170	173	167	172	172	174
175	165	167	172	172	174	166
168	166	171	174	169	172	169.

Check that:

(i)   the greatest height is 175 cm,

(ii)   the least height is 165 cm, and that

(iii)   the height in between these two is 170 cm.

(iv)   The best way to find the most common height is to make a frequency table (see opposite page).

Do you agree that the most common height is 172 cm?

Height	Tally	Total frequency
165	I	1
166	II	2
167	III	3
168	I	1
169	II	2
170	I	1
171	I	1
172	++++	5
173	I	1
174	III	3
175	I	1
		21

(v) If we arrange the heights in order of size, least to greatest, we get:

165, 166, 166, 167, 167, 167, 168, 169, 169, 170, 171, 172, 172, 172, 172, 172, 173, 174. 174, 174, 175.

Check that 171 cm is the height in the middle.

(vi) If we add up all the heights and divide by the number of girls, we get:

$$\frac{165+166+166+167+167+167+168+169+169+170+171+172+172+172+172+172+173+174+174+174+175}{21}$$

$$= \frac{3575}{21} = 170\frac{5}{21} \text{ cm.}$$

How does this value differ from the others?
It does take longer to work out, but it is the most important mathematically.

Which of the six representative values would *you* choose as being the *most typical of the whole group* and why? (It is not an easy choice and you may not all agree.)
However, nobody *should* have chosen 165 cm or 175 cm. Why?
Would you generally expect Method (iii) to give you a representative value that was typical of all the other values? To help you, look at the following shoe sizes taken by a set of second form pupils.

2, 2½, 3, 3, 3½, 4, 4, 4, 4, 4½, 4½, 4½, 4½, 4½, 5, 5, 5, 5, 5, 5, 5, 5½, 5½, 6, 6, 6, 6.

You will have realized that it is not straightforward to know which method to use in choosing a typical or representative value for the group. We need to look at the various possibilities in more detail.

2. THE MODE

Projects

1. From any six 'pop' records choose your favourite. Count the number of votes given to each record. Which is the most popular?

2. Work out your age in months, correct to the nearest month, and make a frequency table for the whole class. What is the most common age?

3. Make a frequency table to show the sizes of shoes taken by your class. Which size occurs most frequently? Would it be the same for a similar class in a Chinese school?

You have just found a representative value for each collection of values by finding the most popular, common or frequently occurring member. This value is called the *Mode*.
What was the mode in each case?
Is it possible to have more than one mode?

Example 2

In *Book B* there was a survey of how members of 1*a* came to school and the results were shown in a bar chart (see Figure 1).

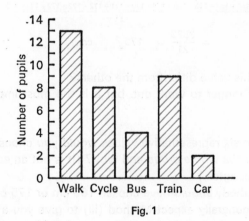

Fig. 1

What is the modal way of coming to school? Why is it easy to find this from a bar chart?
Figure 2 (opposite) shows the same information for a country school. What is the modal way of getting to school this time?
A Head Teacher might use this information when deciding whether to close a school during a bus strike.

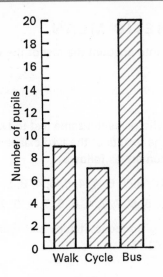

Fig. 2

Exercise A

1   Draw a bar chart to show the number of children in each family in your class. What is the mode?

2   1, 3, 5, 7, 7, 8, 3, 5, 4, 2, 3, 2, 5, 6, 7, 1, 5, 4, 9, 3.
      These numbers are the marks out of ten obtained in a French test. Do you think it was hard? What is the mode?

3   What is the modal height in your class? How does it compare with other classes in the same year in your school?

4   What is the modal record in the current 'Top Ten'? How is the 'Top Ten' worked out?

5   A shopkeeper sold fireworks at various prices. There were 1p ones, 2p ones, etc. He kept a record of the first 60 fireworks bought one day, and their prices in pence were as follows:

1	1	6	3	2	3	6	9	2	4
2	4	6	1	2	4	9	5	4	1
2	2	1	4	5	3	3	9	9	6
1	9	6	4	1	5	2	4	6	2
3	2	1	1	9	6	2	1	1	2
6	1	5	3	1	1	9	1	2	1

Make out the frequency table and find the mode. Which price firework would he least want to keep selling? How much money did he take for each type of firework? Does this affect your answer?

3. THE ARITHMETIC MEAN

Does the mode take into account the rest of the values? Might this often be a disadvantage?

Example 3

Consider a teacher who gives the same test to two different classes; and wishes to compare the results of the two classes.

The marks out of ten are as follows:

Class *A*: 4, 5, 6, 9, 10, 8, 7, 6, 4, 4, 8, 5, 4, 8, 9, 5, 4, 6, 10, 8;

Class *B*: 3, 8, 5, 4, 5, 5, 6, 7, 7, 4, 6, 6, 7, 4, 6, 7, 5, 4, 3, 7, 5, 7, 8, 3.

He starts by making frequency tables and then draws two bar charts. (Figures 3(*a*) and (*b*)).

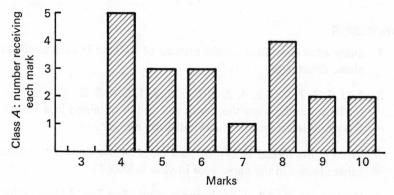

Fig. 3 (*a*)

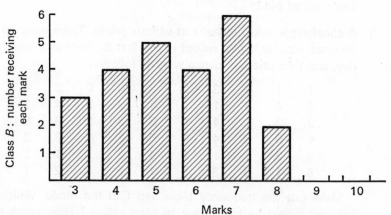

Fig. 3 (*b*)

What is the mode in each class? Discuss whether the modal values are typical or good representatives of the marks of each class. Do they give a fair comparison between each class?

When the schoolmaster adds up the marks obtained by each class he finds that the total for A is 130

and for B is 132.

Why aren't these totals useful for a comparison?

If we were to divide

130 by 20 (the number of pupils in Class A)

and   132 by 24 (the number of pupils in Class B),

would this be better?

$$130 \div 20 = 6\tfrac{10}{20} \quad \text{or} \quad 6\tfrac{1}{2}$$

and

$$132 \div 24 = 5\tfrac{12}{24} \quad \text{or} \quad 5\tfrac{1}{2}.$$

The popular name for the values we have just calculated is 'average'. The mathematical name is *Arithmetic Mean* or simply *Mean*. The mean (or mean value) of Class A is $6\tfrac{1}{2}$. What is the mean of Class B? Do these seem good representative values?

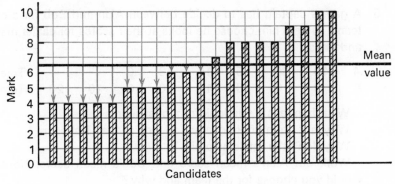

Fig. 4

Figure 4 shows how Class A's marks are arranged in relation to the mean value of $6\tfrac{1}{2}$. How many pupils received marks above it and how many below?

What do the red arrowed lines above and below the mean value line represent?

The total length of the red arrows below this line is given by

$$(2\tfrac{1}{2} \times 5) + (1\tfrac{1}{2} \times 3) + (\tfrac{1}{2} \times 3)$$

$$= \quad 12\tfrac{1}{2} \quad + \quad 4\tfrac{1}{2} \quad + \quad 1\tfrac{1}{2}$$

$$= \quad 18\tfrac{1}{2}.$$

What would you expect the total length of the arrows above the line to be? Work it out. Can you explain your result?

Draw a similar diagram showing Class *B*'s marks. Calculate the total lengths of the arrows above and below the mean value line. What do you find?

Exercise B

1   Find the mean of

(a)   5, 2, 1, 8, 9, 6, 10, 7;
(b)   4, 6, 8, 3, 5, 2, 1, 9, 10;
(c)   5, 6, 4, 0, 3, 0, 2, 8.

2   Peter throws 5, 15, 24, 25, 3, 4, with 6 darts.
What is the mean score per throw? Why isn't it a whole number?

3   Joan scores 2, 5, 0, 9, 1, 3, 3 goals in 7 netball matches. Calculate the arithmetic mean.

4   Ten packets of sweets contain 18, 16, 20, 19, 17, 16, 20, 19, 20, 18 sweets. What is the mean?

5   A games captain has to decide between Alan and Bob for a cricket team. To help him choose he looks at their scores for earlier matches and finds

| A | 10 | 30 | 5 | 15 | 18 | 0 | — | — | Total 78 |
| B | 0 | 5 | 15 | 10 | 20 | 0 | 10 | 20 | Total 80 |

What happens if you look for modal scores?
Why is it not a good idea just to look at their last score?
Why don't the totals help him?
Work out Alan's mean score and Bob's mean score. Now who would you choose for the team and why?

6   What is the mean number of children in the families in your class? How does this compare with the modal number which you have found before?

7   Calculate the arithmetic mean of the numbers 2, 4, 6, 8, 3, 7.
Calculate also the arithmetic mean of the numbers 102, 104, 106, 108, 103, 107. What do you notice?
Write down the arithmetic mean of 72, 74, 76, 78, 73, 77 and of 1442, 1444, 1446, 1448, 1443, 1447.

8   Calculate the arithmetic mean of 715, 718, 714, 717, 716, 717, 710, 719, 711.

9 Find the mean of

(a) 2007, 2012, 2001, 2002, 2008, 2003, 2004;

(b) 991, 993, 995, 992, 990, 997, 999, 1000, 998.

10 (a) Calculate the mean of 1, 2, 2, 3, 5, 5, 5, 6, 7, 9.

(b) What is the mean of each of the following?

(i) 4, 5, 5, 6, 8, 8, 8, 9, 10, 12;

(ii) 2, 4, 4, 6, 10, 10, 10, 12, 14, 18;

(iii) 0, 1, 1, 2, 4, 4, 4, 5, 6, 8;

(iv) 3, 6, 6, 9, 15, 15, 15, 18, 21, 27;

(v) $^-2$, $^-1$, $^-1$, 0, $^+2$, $^+2$, $^+2$, $^+3$, $^+4$, $^+6$.

11 Find the mean of

(a) $^-5$, $^-4$, $^+3$, $^+8$, $^-2$, $^+9$, $^-1$, $^-2$, $^+3$;

(b) $^-6$, $^-5$, $^-3$, $^-2$, 0, $^+3$, $^+4$, $^+7$, $^+11$;

(c) $\frac{1}{2}$, $1\frac{1}{4}$, $\frac{1}{4}$, 1, $1\frac{1}{2}$, $1\frac{3}{4}$, $\frac{3}{4}$, 1.

12 The arithmetic mean of 12 numbers is 7, What can you say about their sum?

13 The mean age of a group of 24 girls is 12 years 1 month. What is the sum of their combined ages?

4. THE MEDIAN

We have seen that the arithmetic mean has two main disadvantages:

(a) it can take a long time to work out;

(b) it is unduly affected by freak values.

So now let us look for a representative value which does *not* have these disadvantages.

Example 4

A form master counted the number of half-days each pupil in his form was absent and arranged them in increasing order as follows:

0, 0, 0, 1, 1, 1, 1, 1, 1, 2, 2, 2, 2, 2, 3, 3, 3, 3,

4, 4, 5, 6, 6, 6, 7, 8, 10, 10, 80, 90.

What number of half-days absence is the mode?

What is the mean?

Why isn't the mean a good type of average to quote here?

How do these figures compare with your own form?

What could account for the long absence of two pupils?

Would you agree that neither the mode nor the mean gives the master a value which is typical of all the others?

He has arranged the numbers in order. What is the middle value?

Is the middle value more typical of these numbers than the mode or the mean?

Middle
value

0, 0, 0, 1, 1, 1, 1, 1, 1, 2, 2, 2, 2, 3, ③,3, 3, 4, 4, 5, 6, 6, 6, 7, 8,10,10,80,90

←——————————→ ←——————————→
14 values   Median   14 values

Fig. 5

This middle value, 3, is called the *Median* (or the median value). What can you say about the number of values before it and the number after it?

What is the median value of

(a) 2, 4, 1, 7, 5;

(b) 3, 6, 6, 5, 7, 1, 8;

(c) 25, 28, 29, 26, 30, 27, 29, 24, 22;

(d) 1, 2, 3, 3, 4, 5;

(e) 1, 2, 3, 4, 5, 6?

What problem do you find with (d) and (e)?

In (d), the two middle numbers are both three, so the median is 3.

In (e), the two middle numbers are 3 and 4. The number half-way between them (the mean of 3 and 4) is $3\frac{1}{2}$. This is the median for (e).

Notice that in (e), the median number is not one of the original numbers.

Find the median mark obtained by the Classes A and B of Section 3. Comment on your results.

Example 5

The drawing shows six boys arranged in ascending order of weight. If we want to find their median weight, whose weight do we need to know?

Chris   Dan   Eddie   Fred   Gerry   Harry

158

Suppose that Eddie weighs 52 kg and Fred 57 kg.

Discuss how to find the weight that is exactly half-way between 52 kg and 57 kg.

Exercise C

1 Arrange each of the following in order of size and find the median.

  (*a*) 7, 6, 1, 2, 5, 8, 3;

  (*b*) 3, 1, 6, 3, 2, 4;

  (*c*) 4, 8, 9, 1, 2, 5, 7, 3, 4, 10;

  (*d*) 21, 25, 31, 28, 22, 29, 24, 30.

2 Find the median height of pupils in your form. How does it compare with the mode and the mean?

3 Find the median shoe size taken by the pupils in your class. How does it compare with the mode?

  Would the manager of a shoe shop prefer to know the modal or the median size of shoe taken by pupils from the local secondary schools? Why?

Summary

When working with statistics it is often useful to be able to choose one representative value. This representative value must be typical of all the values and is often called an *average*.

There are three main types of average:

(*a*) *the mode*—the most frequently occurring item;

(*b*) *the arithmetic mean*—the sum of all the values divided by the number of values;

(*c*) *the median*—the middle value, once the values have been arranged in order of size.

You will have seen that all three types of average have their advantages *and* disadvantages. The choice of a typical value from a collection of values depends on

  (i) the collection of values itself, and

  (ii) the use for which you want an average.

Miscellaneous Exercise D

1 The modal weight of 30 boys is 75 kg. What, if anything, can you say about their total weight?

Would you be able to say anything about their total weight if you were told

(a) their mean weight,

(b) their median weight?

2 Mary knows her own mark in the history examination and also the mode, mean and median of the marks for the whole form. Which average would help her find out whether she came in the 'top' or 'bottom' half of the form?

3 Which of the three types of average need not have a numerical value? Give some examples.

4 In the tiny village of Chatterton there are only ten men of working age. They are listed below together with their annual income.

	Annual income in £'s
The Landowner	10 000
The Farm Manager	1 000
Innkeeper	950
Postmaster	900
Rod	700
Dick	650
David } Farm labourers	600
Ken	500
Peter	500
Brian, the errand boy	400

What is the mean income of the men in the village?

Why is this such a misleading value?

Would the median income be a better one to quote?

Calculate the mean income of the men in the village leaving out the landowner's income from the calculation. Does this give you a better idea of the 'average' income of the men in the village?

5 A manufacturing firm employs 1000 people of which 990 earn less than £18 per week and 10 earn more than £100 per week. If both the median and mean wage were known which would you quote if you were (a) a shop steward; (b) the managing director?

6 If you have made a total of 20 runs in your first 4 innings of the season, how many runs must you make in your fifth innings to double your 'average'? (You are out each time.)

7   In a certain class, 2 children had 5 uncles, 3 had 4, 7 had 3, 4 had 2, 10 had 1, while 14 had no uncles at all. Find the mode and the mean number of uncles per child. Which sort of average is most suitable in this case?

8   The bar chart in Figure 6 illustrates information gathered about the number of sisters of the boys in a certain group. No boy had more than 5 sisters.

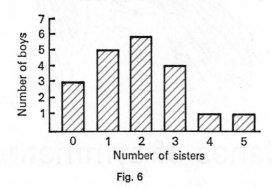

Fig. 6

    (a)   How many boys are there in this group?

    (b)   What is the modal number of sisters?

    (c)   What is the mean number of sisters?

    (d)   Is it more useful to talk about the mean or the mode in this case?
Why?

9   Taking M to represent (i) mode, (ii) mean, (iii) median, say whether each of the above statements are always, sometimes or never true.

    (a)   The M is one of the actual readings.

    (b)   The M can be the greatest or least reading.

    (c)   When the readings are arranged in order of size, the M has as many numbers before it as after it.

    (d)   One or two freak readings may unduly bias the M.

    (e)   The M can have more than one value.

12. Planes of symmetry

Experiment 1

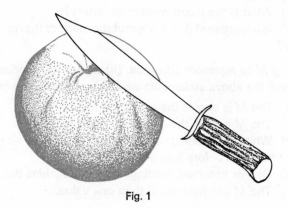

Fig. 1

Get a good round apple. Remove the stalk. Cut the apple in half. Take one half and place the cut against a shiny metal surface, such as the inside of a tin lid. What do you see?

Experiment 2

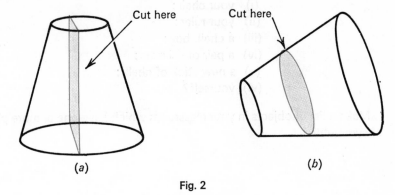

(a)　　　　　　　　　(b)

Fig. 2

Cut a large cork into two parts as shown in Figure 2 (*a*). (Your teacher may have some corks which have already been cut.) Take each part in turn and place the cut against a shiny metal surface. What do you see? Repeat the experiment with a cut as shown in Figure 2 (*b*).

Experiment 3

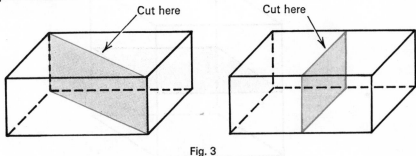

Fig. 3

Repeat Experiment 2 using a rectangular bar of soap cut into two parts as shown in Figures 3 (*a*) and (*b*).

When you placed the red cut or section in Figure 2 (*a*) against a shiny metal surface, you should have seen one whole cork. We say that the red section lies in a *plane of symmetry*.

(*a*) Does the red section in Figure 2(*b*) lie in a plane of symmetry?

(*b*) Did you cut the apple along a plane of symmetry?

(*c*) Which of the red sections in Figure 3 lie in a plane of symmetry of the bar of soap?

(*d*) Does the bar of soap have any other planes of symmetry?

163

(e) How many planes of symmetry has:

       (i) your chair;
     (ii) your ruler;
    (iii) a chalk box;
    (iv) a pair of scissors;
     (v) a new stick of chalk;
    (vi) yourself?

Make a list of objects in your classroom which have one or more planes of symmetry.

Experiment 4

For this experiment you will need straws cut into lengths of 10 cm, pipe cleaners, card and glue.

Make a skeleton cube from the straws and pipe cleaners.

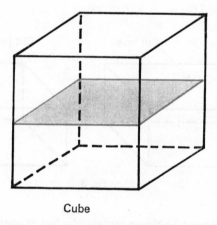

Cube

Fig. 4

Look at Figure 4. On your cube, what shape is the red section? What size is it? Cut the section from card and glue it in the position shown. Does the section lie in a plane of symmetry of the cube? Describe in your own words the position of this plane of symmetry.

Does the cube have other planes of symmetry which pass through the mid-points of four edges? How many? Make skeleton models to show these.

On your cube, what shape is the red section shown in Figure 5? See if you can make one which is the right size to fit your model. Make a new skeleton cube. Cut the rectangular section from card and glue it in position.

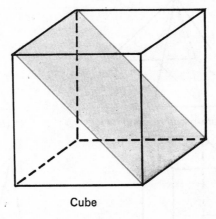

Cube

Fig. 5

Does this section lie in a plane of symmetry? If so, describe it in your own words. Are there other planes of symmetry like this? Make skeleton models to show these. Ask your friends to help you.

How many planes of symmetry do you think a cube has?

Exercise A

1   How many planes of symmetry has:

(*a*) the tray of a match-box;

(*b*) a shoe;

(*c*) a pair of glasses;

(*d*) a jam jar?

Make a list of objects in your home which have a plane of symmetry.

2   Many parts of a car are made so that one is the mirror image of the other, for example, the wings covering the wheels. Name as many parts as you can which are made in this way?

The driver's door is damaged and has to be replaced. Will a passenger's door fit?

Does a car have a plane of symmetry? Give your reasons.

165

3 Which of the red sections shown in Figure 6 lie in planes of symmetry? (If you find this question difficult, make skeleton models.)

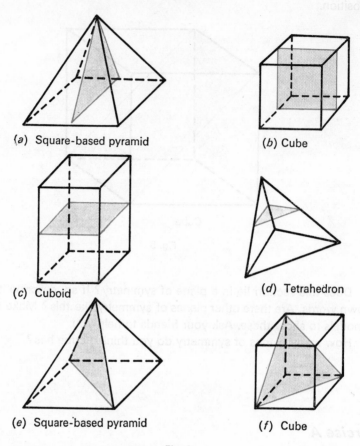

(a) Square-based pyramid

(b) Cube

(c) Cuboid

(d) Tetrahedron

(e) Square-based pyramid

(f) Cube

Fig. 6

4 Place the following objects on a shiny metal surface and describe the new shape which appears:

(a) a cube;

(b) a cuboid;

(c) a hemisphere (on its circular face);

(d) a cylinder (on one of its circular ends);

(e) a cone (on its circular face);

(f) a square-based pyramid (on its square base).

5 How many planes of symmetry has:

(*a*) a square-based pyramid;
(*b*) a cylinder;
(*c*) a cube;
(*d*) a cone;
(*e*) an equilateral triangular prism?

6

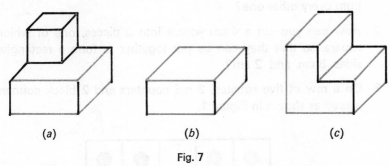

(*a*)   (*b*)   (*c*)

Fig. 7

In Figure 7, the red line segments represent lengths of 6 cm and the black line segments represent lengths of 3 cm. How many planes of symmetry has each of the three solids shown?

7 How many planes of symmetry has (*a*) a sphere, (*b*) a hemisphere? Does a sphere have more planes of symmetry than a hemisphere?

8 Look at a pair of semi-detached houses. Do they have a plane of symmetry?

Exercise B. Class projects

1 How many planes of symmetry has:

(*a*) a regular tetrahedron;
(*b*) a regular octahedron?

Make a set of skeleton models which shows these planes of symmetry.

2 Collect objects in common use and classify them according to the number of planes of symmetry which they have. Make a classroom display.

Puzzle corner

1 How can four points be arranged so that each is the same distance from every other one?

2 How can you cut a 4 cm square into 3 pieces, one of which is a square, so that they can be put together to form a rectangle with sides 8 cm and 2 cm?

3 On a row of five squares, 2 red counters and 2 black counters are placed as shown in Figure 1.

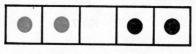

Fig. 1

How can you get the red counters in the places originally occupied by the black, and vice versa, if only the moves and hops shown in Figure 2 are allowed?

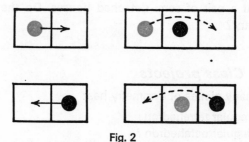

Fig. 2

4 Remove 3 matches from the 15 shown in Figure 3 so that only 3 squares are left.

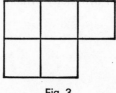

Fig. 3

5   If *a*, *b*, *c* are consecutive numbers and

$$\begin{array}{r} a\ b\ c \\ +c\ b\ a\,, \\ \hline d\ d\ d \end{array} \quad \text{find } a, b, c, d.$$

6   29121291911818922914720151315181523.

Crack this code, if the first 26 counting numbers represent the letters of the alphabet: $A = 1$, $B = 2$, $C = 3$, etc.

7   A paper boy delivers 28 copies of *The Daily Telegraph*, 24 copies of *The Times* and 20 copies of the *Daily Express* in a street of 50 houses.

Assuming that no house receives more than 2 papers, or 2 identical papers, what is

(*a*) the smallest number of houses which could have two papers delivered;

(*b*) the largest number of houses which could have two papers delivered?

8

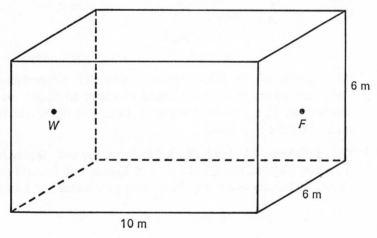

Fig. 4

In a room measuring 10 m by 6 m by 6 m, a fly, *F*, is sitting in the middle of one wall and a wasp, *W*, in the middle of the opposite one (see Figure 4).

The wasp catches the fly by *crawling* all the way to it while the fly, paralysed by fear, remains still. Find the shortest route that the wasp can take. How long is it?

[*Hint:* by first drawing a suitable net, make a scale model of the room (but do not stick it together) and mark the position of the fly and the wasp.]

9 Six girls want to play tennis (singles). In how many ways can they pair off?

10 A showman was travelling with a wolf, a goat and a basket of cabbages. He did not dare leave the wolf with the goat or the goat with the cabbages. On coming to a river he was faced with the problem of ferrying them across using a boat which would only carry himself and one of them at a time. How did he get them across?

11 A goods train leaves Retford for London at the same time as a passenger express leaves London for Retford. If the goods train travels at 50 km/h and the express at 100 km/h, which is the nearer to London when they meet?
(Assume that London is 200 km from Retford.)

12

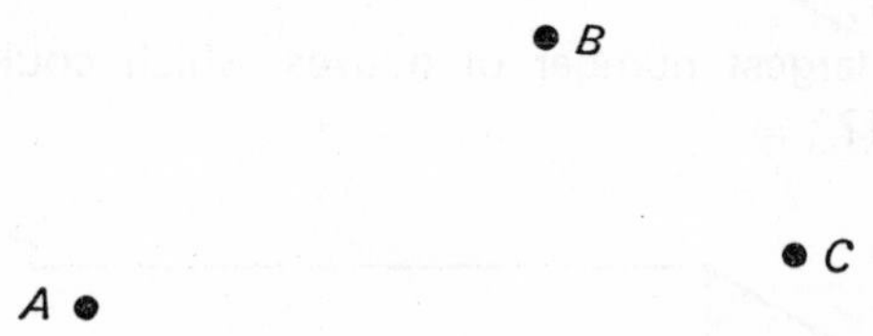

● *B*

● *C*

A ●

Fig. 5

When a ship sank, the only 3 survivors swam off in different directions. They each swam at the same speed and after an hour were at the positions *A*, *B*, *C* shown in Figure 5. Copy this figure and find the spot where the ship sank.

13 Out of 30 boys, 24 play football, 18 play rugby and 10 play hockey. If no boy plays all three, but four play hockey and football and four more play hockey and rugby, how many play football and rugby?

Revision exercises

Quick quiz, no. 3

1 Write down a negative rotation which has the same effect as a rotation of $^+240°$.

2 The figure shows a cube with a right pyramid fitted on top. How many planes of symmetry has the solid?

3 What is the mean of 12, 13, 14, 15, 16?

4 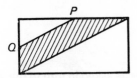 *P* and *Q* are the middle points of two sides of a rectangle. What fraction of the rectangle is shaded?

5 Find the values of
   (*a*) $^-7+^-3$; (*b*) $^-7-^-3$; (*c*) $^-3-^-7$.

6 *X* is due east of *A* and *Y* is due north of *A*. What is the bearing of *X* from *Y*?

Quick quiz, no. 4

1 Name two quadrilaterals that have just two lines of symmetry.

2 Arrange these directed numbers in order of size and find their median:

$$^+8, \quad ^-6, \quad 0, \quad ^+5, \quad ^+2, \quad ^-4.$$

3 Onto what point is ($^+2$, $^+3$) mapped by a half-turn about the origin?

4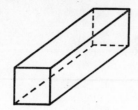

How many planes of symmetry has this rectangular box with square ends?

5 Calculate, leaving your answers in powers of 2:

(a) $2^8 \times 2^2$;   (b) $2^0 \times 2^2 \times 2^4$;   (c) $2^7 \div 2^3$.

6

How are the following triangles related to triangle *A*?

(a) triangle *B*;   (b) triangle *C*.

Exercise C

1 Each member of a group of twenty girls was asked in turn to guess how many peas there were in a certain match box. Their guesses were as follows:

105, 100, 90, 88, 76, 102, 98, 97, 106, 98, 79, 85, 98, 100, 101, 103, 95, 98, 104, 100.

What was the modal guess?
Calculate the arithmetic mean of the guesses.

2

Copy Figure 1, letter all the nodes and find a route matrix to describe it. Is the figure traversable? Colour the figure using as few colours as possible, so that each region is a different colour from the one next to it.

Fig. 1

172

3 The coordinates of the vertices of a triangle are ($^+$1, 0), ($^+$4, 0), ($^+$4, $^+$2).

(*a*) Plot these on squared paper and draw the triangle T_1.
(*b*) Reflect T_1 in the $y = 0$ axis and draw its image T_2.
(*c*) Reflect T_2 in the $x = 0$ axis and draw its image T_3.
(*d*) Reflect T_3 in the line $y = x$ and draw its image T_4.

How is T_1 related to T_3 and T_4?

4 The course of a ship after leaving a port P is as follows:

40 km, bearing 040°,

followed by 90 km, bearing 080°.

Find by accurate drawing:

(*a*) the distance of the ship from the port;
(*b*) the bearing of the ship from the port;
(*c*) the bearing of the port from the ship.

5 *A, B, C, D* are four identical flags.

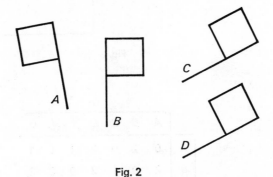

Fig. 2

(*a*) Which of the flags can be mapped onto D by a single rotation?
(*b*) Which of the flags can be mapped onto A by a single rotation?
(*c*) Find the angles and centres of rotation wherever possible.

Exercise D

1 Use the scales you made in Chapter 9 to do the following calculations:

(*a*) 6×8;   (*b*) 14×3;   (*c*) $3\frac{1}{2} \times 4$;   (*d*) $1\frac{3}{4} \times 8$;

(*e*) $88 \div 8$;   (*f*) $18 \div 4$;   (*g*) $4\frac{1}{2} \div 2$;   (*h*) $3\frac{1}{2} \div \frac{1}{2}$.

2 A manufacturing firm produces 70 tonnes of a certain product in one year and 45 tonnes in the next year. How much must it produce in the third year to give a mean of 60 tonnes over the three years?

3 Trace Figure 3. The squares are related by rotations about A and B. Describe fully these relations between S and S_1.
Can S be mapped onto S_1 by a rotation about any other point?
Are the squares related in any other ways?

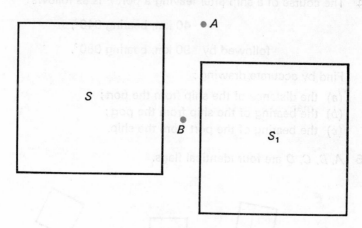

Fig. 3

4

From		To						
		A	*B*	*C*	*D*	*E*	*F*	*G*
	A	0	2	0	3	1	1	1
	B	2	0	1	2	0	0	3
	C	0	1	0	4	1	2	3
	D	3	2	4	0	0	1	1
	E	1	0	1	0	0	0	2
	F	1	0	2	1	0	0	4
	G	1	3	3	1	2	4	0

This route matrix describes a very complicated network. Without drawing the network, describe it in as much detail as you can and say whether it is traversable.

5

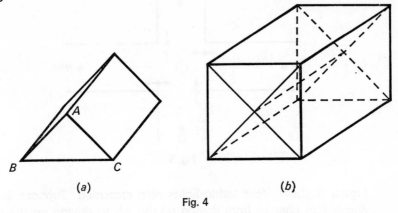

(a)   *(b)*

Fig. 4

How many planes of symmetry has the isosceles triangular prism in Figure 4(*a*)? If four of these prisms can be put together to form the square-based prism in Figure 4(*b*), what can you say about triangle *ABC*? How many planes of symmetry has the solid in Figure 4 (*b*)?

Exercise E

1 Draw the quadrilaterals with vertices as follows:

    (*a*) ($^-$3, 0), ($^-$1, $^+$1), ($^+$1, 0), ($^-$1, $^-$3);

    (*b*) ($^-$3, $^+$1), ($^-$3, $^-$1), ($^+$1, $^-$1), ($^+$1, $^+$1);

    (*c*) ($^+$1, $^+$2), (0, 0), ($^-$5, 0), ($^-$4, $^+$2).

(i) Give the special name of each quadrilateral.

(ii) Draw in any lines of symmetry and state their equation(s).

2 Complete the following:

$$2^2 = ?, \qquad 1 \times 3 = ?,$$
$$3^2 = ?, \qquad 2 \times 4 = ?,$$
$$5^2 = ?, \qquad 4 \times 6 = ?,$$
$$8^2 = ?, \qquad 7 \times 9 = ?,$$
$$11^2 = ?, \qquad 10 \times 12 = ?,$$
$$n^2 = ?, \qquad ? \times ? = ?.$$

Use the pattern to work out

    (*a*) 19×21;

    (*b*) 49×51;

    (*c*) 299×301.

3

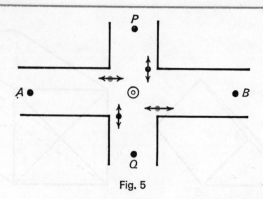

Fig. 5

Figure 5 shows four traffic lights at a crossroad. Suppose Britain decided to change from driving on the left to driving on the right. Which of the following changes of position would produce the necessary rearrangement of the lights?

(*a*) Rotation through 180° about ◎;

(*b*) rotation through ⁻90 or ⁺90 about ◎;

(*c*) reflection in *PQ* only;

(*d*) reflection in *AB* only;

(*e*) reflection in *AB* or *PQ*.

4

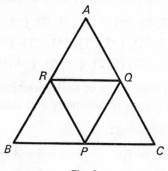

Fig. 6

The four small equilateral triangles in Figure 6 are the same size. If *BP* is *a* cm long and triangle *BRP* has area *A* cm², give expressions for the following:

(*a*) the length of *RQ*;

(*b*) the length of *BC*;

(*c*) the area of triangle *ARQ*;

(*d*) the area of triangle *ABC*.

   In what mirror line is *P* the image of *A*?

   How many lines of symmetry has the figure?

5 Find four different changes of position which will map triangle *RBP* onto triangle *PQC* in Figure 6.

Exercise F

Complete this cross-number.

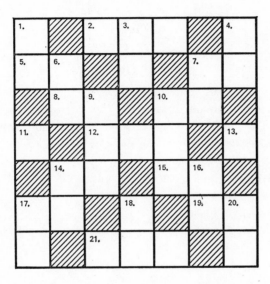

<table>
<tr><td>Clues Across</td><td>Clues Down</td></tr>
</table>

Clues Across

2. $4875 \div 15$.
5. 82·6 correct to 2 S.F.
7. $\dfrac{8}{9} = \dfrac{?}{72}$.
8. $^{+}31 + {}^{-}9$.
10. How many vertices has a hexagonal prism?
11. A cuboid with square ends has ? planes of symmetry.
12. $9 \cdot 8 \times 40$.
13. A cube has ? planes of symmetry.
14. The image of 9 under the mapping $x \to 20 - x$.
15. The fifth prime number.
17. The length (in cm) of a side of a square of area 625 cm².
19. 2^5.
21. $110 \times 1 \cdot 2$.

Clues Down

1. $72_{\text{eight}} = ?_{\text{ten}}$.
3. $^{+}12 - {}^{-}8$.
4. An octagonal prism has ? edges.
6. The difference between £9·81 and £9·49 in pence.
7. 5, 12, 20, 29, 39, 50, ?.
9. $4620 \div 20$.
10. $22_{\text{five}} \times 3_{\text{five}} = ?_{\text{five}}$.
14. How many degrees is $\frac{1}{6}$ of a right-angle?
16. $63 - 47 = 19$ in what number base?
17. How many members has {multiples of 4 < 100}?
18. 28·68 + 53·87 correct to 2 S.F.
20. A right-angled triangle has sides 6 cm, 8 cm, 10 cm. What is its area in cm²?

Find four different changes of position which will map triangle PQR onto triangle PQC in Figure 5.

Exercise F

Complete this cross number.

Clues Across

Clues Down